WILLIAM
Dobell

1 Self-portrait, 1968 (unfinished)

WILLIAM
Dobell

A BIOGRAPHICAL AND CRITICAL STUDY BY JAMES GLEESON

Angus & Robertson Publishers

2 Dobell in his studio

ANGUS & ROBERTSON PUBLISHERS
London ● Sydney ● Melbourne ● Singapore ● Manila

This edition first published by Angus & Robertson Publishers, Australia, 1981
Published by arrangement with Thames and Hudson Limited, London

© James Gleeson 1964, 1969, 1981

National Library of Australia
Cataloguing-in-publication data.

Gleeson, James, 1915-
    William Dobell.
    Rev. ed.
    Includes index.
    ISBN 0 207 14007 3.

    1. Dobell, Sir William, 1899-1970. 2. Painting,
    Australian. I. Dobell, Sir William, 1899-1970.
    II. Title.

759.994

Typeset in 12pt Bembo
Printed in Hong Kong

Contents

Foreword to the 1981 Edition

William Dobell died at the age of seventy on 14 May 1970, barely a year after the revised edition of 1969. I have not attempted to bring that text into the present by re-wording it in the past tense, and to add a brief appendix, in the past tense, on the works of his last months seemed inappropriate.

Yet something must be said about these late works because a number of them are of real consequence in his *oeuvre*. Examination of final fruits in a foreword may seem paradoxical but it can be justified on the ground that it also serves as a summing up of the position he had finally reached as an artist.

As time ran out he was preoccupied with two major problems — how to paint himself and how to paint a second portrait of Thelma Clune.

Some time in 1965 he was persuaded to accept a commission to paint a self-portrait for a collection of Australian painting being formed for the American collector Harold Mertz. He needed to be persuaded because he realised all too well that the task of painting a self-portrait that would satisfy his own exacting demands would be a very taxing one, and unlike Rembrandt, he had never been really interested in tracing out his own experiences and measuring the onslaughts of time as they were mirrored in his changing appearance.

So the process began. In all there were three preparatory pencil drawings and six painted versions of the self-portrait, and even in the version which fate decreed was to be the final one, he felt he had not arrived at a completely satisfactory solution. In the last conversation I had with him he said he was not quite happy with it and would try again.

This restless search for the truth is a characteristic of Dobell's whole approach to portraiture. He would never accept a near miss. If something in the character of the sitter eluded him he would come back to it again and again until he felt he had reached the truth.

Only two of the six versions had a public history before his death. The unsigned and undated 'final' version was shown in his last exhibition at Newcastle a month before he died, and an earlier, smaller version signed and dated 1966 was exhibited with the Mertz Collection at the Adelaide Festival of that year.

The 'final' version was reproduced as the frontispiece in the 1969 edition of this book, and again now.

The signed version was a good likeness and an excitingly painted painting. Why did he feel it had failed?

In all probability it was the very stylishness of the painting that upset him. It was a *bravura* piece. Every stroke, every accent was put down incisively and with absolute confidence, and this created an impression that was at variance with the real truth. He could be confident and incisive with paint because he had become its master, but in his own nature he was shy, sensitive, hesitant, reluctant and slow to make decisions. He knew that the *brio* and virtuosity of the painting was not a true indication of his nature — and the one virtue of portraiture, as he saw it, was to come as close to the truth as possible.

The penultimate version, now in the Art Gallery of South Australia, is probably the most remarkable of the whole sequence.

It is tempting to assume that it was painted during the last illness or after the death of his sister Alice, who had been his companion and housekeeper for almost a quarter of a century.

The quizzical look and the half smile of the Mertz study are gone. Here the eyes are open but they see nothing, because his thoughts have turned inwards. He is not studying his reflection in a mirror but reflecting inwardly on matters that are beyond remedy. Whatever it is that his mind is fixed upon has stripped his features of the usual defences used in presenting a public front. All the mechanisms and mannerisms which shield the inner self against the abrasions of social intercourse are here removed and the spirit is exposed and naked.

We see a Dobell we would never have known in real life because we would never have been permitted to look so deeply into his soul. Only once, in the privacy of this most personal portrait, did he lower his guard and paint the quiet despair, the acceptance of hopelessness, the anguished quietude of his old age.

Exuberant stylishness had made the Mertz study psychologically false; now he had painted a portrait that was too private, and too revealing. What he needed was a compromise, a portrait that would be psychologically accurate yet at the same time have the qualities he considered necessary in a public image of himself. Hence the 'final' version which followed the study into the Mertz Collection after his death.

The second portrait of Thelma Clune was painted in the last months of his life, and is still held by the foundation set up under the terms of Dobell's will.

It must be regarded as a painting stemming from a second crisis of confidence — the first being caused by the court case of 1944, the second resulting from a serious illness in 1957 and from a feeling that he had been left behind by the changing fashions of art.

For the first time in a major work he introduced semi-abstract elements, and the ensuing compound is one of the most vivacious, perceptive and daring portraits he ever painted.

It is true that there are unresolved formal problems in this work, problems that he would surely have solved had he been spared to continue with it. The relationship between the realist-expressive element and the abstract-expressive element lacks the fine tuning that would certainly have come with a final consideration.

Nevertheless, it is one of the most authentic portraits he ever painted and as his last major work it stands as a signpost pointing in the direction he would have taken. At the end he was still an explorer trying to find new ways to the truth that lies behind the facade of human appearance.

Introduction

No artist is so great that his greatness is not confined by limits.

There are legitimate criticisms that can be levelled against the art of William Dobell, though more often than not these criticisms merely serve to define the limits of his excellence. It is true to say that his contribution is of a kind that will not affect the subsequent course of art. Goya would not have been astonished by his style or unfamiliar with his attitude. Rembrandt would have understood his intentions.

Nowadays it is rare for a great artist to stand anywhere except at the vanguard of a movement. Dobell is an exception. He has looked closely at Soutine and the Expressionists, at Renoir and the Impressionists, and at some of the older masters, but his true involvement is with humanity. Fashionable trends and recent theories have failed to divert him from his Dickensian interest in the uniqueness of the individual and the mystery of personality.

The best of his portraits have no superiors in twentieth-century art and only Kokoschka can match his skill in revealing the spirit beneath the skin.

Since behaviour is an expression of the personality in action, he is fascinated by genre subjects. London and Sydney have provided him with a richly varied cast of actors whom he catches in situations of comedy or tragedy or, more frequently, at those aimless, unmemorable moments that seem to sum up a way of life.

Though his observation can sometimes be ruthlessly exact he is not a social critic in the tradition of Hogarth or Daumier. He is not out to reform a condition by underlining the stupidity or evil inherent in it. If this is a limitation then it is a most amiable one, for it is due to a sense of humility that prevents him from assuming the role of judge. Still less are his observations weakened by a mawkish brand of pity. There is too much of Rabelais and Rowlandson in his make-up to allow his sympathy ever to spill over into sentimentality. His sharp eye loves to deflate pretentiousness and he will invariably discover a ridiculous needle in a haystack of common sense. The freshness of his approach lies in the fact that he never seems to take the attitude that it was clever of him to detect the pretence and that it was a moral duty to deflate it. Unlike most zealous reformers who act as though they stood outside and above the human situation and are intent upon chipping at it until it is shaped in their own image, Dobell admits that he is involved in the same situation. He has no axe to grind. He does not act as though he believed a world refashioned to his own standards would necessarily be any better than the world he sees about him.

So, he unfurls no flag to rally a band of followers. In Australia he stands in lonely eminence; his name a household word, his pictures bought at record prices, revered almost as an old master, deeply appreciated but without influence on the present generation of artists.

As in most parts of the Western world today, art in Australia is pursuing a line that takes it further and further away from the principles of humanism on which Dobell's art is based. Man is being eased out of the picture. A new pictorial language has been evolved to allow the artist to express his understanding or intuition about a strange and revolutionary age. If ever a time demanded revolutionary artists, that time is now.

In this sense Dobell has failed to meet the challenge of his time. Yet his art is timeless and one can only shrink from a future incapable of finding itself reflected in his paintings.

Again, in an age impressed by bigness, Dobell's finest works are often little bigger than miniatures. His largest things would be lost in the corner of a Pollock and some of his masterpieces would fit comfortably in a pocket.

The fallacy of assuming that size and content are proportionate to one another is, of course, obvious. Yet it persists. A declining film industry's answer to the challenge of television was to build ever bigger screens, on the assumption that the films would be that much better.

Perhaps it is true that the pace of modern living favours large declamatory works of art – pictures that we can take in 'on the wing' as it were. It may also be true that in the West miniature painting has always had a stigma attached to it, at least since the Renaissance and the development of the printing press. As a minor art it has a place among the souvenirs and keep-sakes. It was naturally assumed that if an artist had something important to say he would say it on a large and important surface.

Dobell felt differently about it. You did not increase the significance of a statement by shouting it. Nor was it necessary to paint an acre in order to achieve an effect of monumentality. A few square inches were all that was needed if the conception itself was monumental.

Nevertheless the stigma existed, and Dobell's reaction to the charge of miniaturism was to force himself to develop a broader and more vigorous style, though he continued to work on relatively small panels.

Again, he defies the labellers who would pin a tag on him and stow him safely beside Nolan and Drysdale on the shelf called 'Nationalism – subdivision, Australian' or, alternatively, on the shelf reserved for the followers of the international style.

Certainly we will be able to discover elements in his work that must be regarded as characteristically Australian, though they are inadvertent, unconsciously formed characteristics, and not the result of deliberate choice. He is equally at home in London, or the highlands of New Guinea, as he is in Sydney and, apart from the landscape near his home at Wangi, he has no interest in the sort of scene that means so much to artists like Nolan, Drysdale, and Boyd. Fundamentally his interest is in people rather than places, and since people vary only marginally from place to place, he finds suitable material wherever he happens to be.

Landscapes, on the other hand, vary enormously, and an artist who concentrates on types of scenery that are peculiar to his country is quickly regarded as a Nationalist painter, though it must be borne in mind that it would be superficial to describe a painting as Australian in character simply because it depicted a characteristically Australian scene. Canaletto and Monet painted pictures of the Thames, but they remained obstinately un-English.

The essential element in a National style is not the subject-matter but a certain spirit that is embodied in the work which can make itself felt in abstract art as clearly as in a landscape. John Olsen's abstracts are no less Australian than the landscapes of Sidney Nolan and Russell Drysdale or, to put it another way, Nolan's and Drysdale's landscapes are no less international than Olsen's abstracts, for both these artists began their careers with a close study of the principles of abstract art, and their subsequent work gained strength from this discipline. The success these two artists have achieved abroad may be attributed partly to the fact that their paintings of the Australian Desert express an emotion that can be instantly understood by European, British, and American alike, for the Desert has become a symbol of man's inner loneliness and sense of isolation. They did not originate the Cult of the Desert. T. S. Eliot had already established it as a potent symbol in *The Waste Land* published in 1922, and it has featured prominently in the paintings of the Surrealists and the neo-Romantics. What they did was to give to the symbol the piquancy of reality. By comparison with these landscapes, Dobell's paintings seem to speak with fewer traces of an Australian accent.

Only after one has studied the pantheon of characters he has chosen to portray does it become clear that they are the product of an attitude that has a distinctive Australian cast to it, and even more revealing than the types themselves is the artist's own attitude to his sitters. Statesmen and labourers are treated with a democratic equality. In fact, his sympathies are more often engaged by workmen, waitresses, and by fellow artists or writers than by heads of state or leaders of society. Sometimes in these latter sorts of portrait he falls into a stilted style, or the forms stiffen in conventional moulds, and there is a feeling of strain never felt in his studies of less exalted sitters.

A roll-call of his greatest portraits tells its own story. *Joshua Smith*, artist; *James Cook*, artist; *Elaine Haxton*, artist; *Margaret Olley*, artist; *Brian Penton*, writer; *Frank Clune*, writer; *Dame Mary Gilmore*, writer; and those anonymous portraits that are no less portraits for being anonymous, *The Sleeping Greek*, waiter; *The Cypriot*, the same waiter; *The Strapper*; *The Student*; *The Billy Boy*; and the *Cement Worker*. Of these, only *The Sleeping Greek* really belongs to the London period. *The Cypriot* was painted in Australia from sketches made in London, and the rest belong to the gallery of Australian types he has created since his return. Until then he seemed more interested in capturing the general characteristics of types than in trying to isolate and define the qualities that give uniqueness even to the most typical.

The Charlady, Mrs South Kensington, Irish Youth, Tired Nippy, The Red Lady, Woman in Restaurant, Boy at the Basin, and *The Little Milliner* are paintings in which he summarizes his experiences of a wide range of human personalities. It is almost as though he was making a catalogue, selecting always and only the faces that most completely embody the characteristics of their class, their temperament, or their condition. Consciously, or intuitively, he was working from the general towards the particular, from the type towards the individual, from the face that mirrors a section of society to the face that is the mirror of a soul.

He is an Australian artist, only because he is Australian by birth and upbringing, because his greatest portraits happen to be of Australians, and because we can detect in his attitude to his sitters an egalitarianism that comports with our conception of our national character.

Stylistically he is a traditionalist. He has absorbed many influences from old and recent masters and transformed them

Ills. 75, 70, 67, 90, 76, 115

Ills. 30, 63, 69, 66, 60

Ills. 24, 25, 23, 19, 31, 12, 27, 17

13

into something entirely his own. Yet we live in an age that has felt itself obliged to reject the past as a reliable guide to the present. It is hard for us to believe that a living artist who is not an ardent revolutionary can have anything of real importance to say. For those whose eyes and sensibilities have been conditioned by the international school to regard all non-conformists as reactionaries, Dobell's art poses a problem. Quite obviously he is a master of his art, yet equally obviously his art seems not of this time. There is a feeling that his pictures should have been painted a century ago, when they would have been both revolutionary and right. We are plagued by the thought that they are anachronistic. Perhaps they are, for history is full of artists who lived before or after the time that was ripe for them. Fra Angelico was an anachronism. Ingres was another; and there have been dozens who arrived before the world was quite ready for them. A hundred years from now it will not matter that they were painted later than they should have been had all the clocks been properly synchronized. If there are still people capable of being stirred by art they will be grateful that they were painted at all.

CHAPTER ONE

The Early Years: 1899–1929

William Dobell was born in a house on the corner of Bull and Corlette Streets, Newcastle, N.S.W., on 24 September 1899 – the son of Robert Dobell and Margaret Emma Wrightson, who had married in Newcastle in 1883. At the time of his birth Robert and Margaret Dobell already had six children, though one daughter had died in infancy. Thus, William found himself the youngest in a family of three girls and three boys.

There is no history of artistic interests or tendencies in his family. His father's occupation is listed as bricklayer in his marriage certificate, and as plasterer in his death certificate of 8 February 1939. His paternal grandfather had been a miner and his maternal grandfather an engine-driver. No background would seem less propitious to the nurturing of an artistic talent, and the relative slowness of his development can probably be attributed to a lack of stimulus at an early age, though his natural skill at drawing did attract attention at Cooks Hill School, and he was encouraged to develop his talent by one of his teachers – John Walker.

Certainly when Dobell did commence a serious study of art he made astonishing progress, but he was twenty-five years old before he enrolled at an art school. His scholastic career was as brief as the law allowed, and in it he showed no particular aptitudes apart from his ability to draw.

There was no art gallery within a hundred miles and the only art class available was a course in free-hand drawing at the local technical college. For a while Dobell attended these classes a few nights each week, drawing plaster ornaments, and in the day-time he worked at anything that came along.

He maintains that one of the first of these casual jobs was 'dog walloping'. In those days drapers used to arrange bolts of cloth on the pavement outside the window and a dog walloper's job was to make sure they did not receive the attentions of incontinent dogs.

Since his father was in the building trade, and since architecture seemed to offer some scope for his love of drawing, it was decided to apprentice him to an architect. In 1916 he entered into articles with the Newcastle architect, Wallace L. Porter.

Eight years later he was offered a job in the draughting office of Wunderlich Limited, a firm in Sydney which manufactured building materials.

For several years he was one of forty or more draughtsmen working on architectural metalwork and terracotta, but his obvious artistic talent led to his transfer to the advertising office where he made drawings for catalogues and newspaper advertisements. He stayed at Wunderlich until May 1929.

The job in Sydney meant that he could now attend a proper art school. In 1924 he enrolled as a night student at the Sydney Art School, later known as the Julian Ashton School. For three nights a week he drew in the company of Douglas Dundas, E. A. Harvey, Rah Fizelle, Harold Abbott, Herbert Badham, Harold Byrne, and John Brackenreg, and on Saturday afternoons he studied painting. John Passmore and Lyndon Dadswell were also students while Dobell was there.

At first his ambition was to become a cartoonist for a newspaper, but Julian Ashton recognized his talent for painting and encouraged him in that direction.

The third decade of the twentieth century was not a creative period in Australian art. On the contrary, both Sydney and Melbourne were dominated by artists who were openly antagonistic towards the modern movement, though the attitude in Sydney was a little more liberal owing to the influence of George Lambert and Sydney Ure Smith.

Impressionism had had its effect early in the 1890s, but no hint of the Post-Impressionist revolution of the 1880s reached Australia until the eve of the First World War – a time lag of thirty years. Even then its influence was slight and the new ideas made little headway until the 1930s, by which time Dobell was in England.

In 1913 Norah Simpson brought back from Europe colour reproductions, photographs and books that were to have a decisive effect on the development of Roland Wakelin, Roy de Maistre, and Grace Cossington Smith. But they were students of the more forward-looking school conducted by Dattilo Rubbo, and it is doubtful if any evidence of the artistic ferment going on in Europe was seriously presented to the students of the more conservative Sydney Art School.

By the time Dobell came to study there, the undisputed arbiter of taste and model of artistic perfection was George Lambert A.R.A., an Australian who had spent the early years of the century in Europe painting with an elegance and bravura that sometimes suggested Sargent. Later, under the influence of Orpen, Lambert's colour became lighter and more highly pitched. His paint lost its juicy richness and became thin and dry, and his drawing, always somewhat mannered and inclined to affectation, became even more so, though he was careful to remain within the limits of the accepted canon.

During the First World War, Lambert had been an official war artist for the A.I.F., and in 1921 he returned to Sydney to complete his war paintings.

He was regarded, and probably regarded himself, as the champion of 'safe' modernism. In Sydney he typified the progressive academician, an artist who could detect the flaws and limitations inherent in the theories of tonal realism preached by Max Meldrum in Melbourne, yet one who was not taken in by the excesses of such cranks as Cézanne, Van Gogh, and Gauguin, and outright charlatans like Picasso and Matisse.

This was the attitude also encouraged by Sydney Ure Smith as Editor of the influential magazine *Art in Australia*, and as President of the Society of Artists, the most important exhibiting society in the country at the time.

Post-Impressionism was welcomed as long as its manners were polite and it did not raise its voice above a conversational level, but not until the end of 1939 was Sydney able to see at first-hand a really representative collection of modern European paintings in the Loan Exhibition sponsored by the Melbourne *Herald*. So Dobell received his initial training in an atmosphere that reflected the standards of the Royal Academy.

In May 1929 he entered a painting called *After the Matinée* for the Australian Art Quest conducted by the newly built State Theatre in Sydney. It was a carefully composed, firmly drawn study of two ballerinas in a dressing-room, and it was awarded a third prize of one hundred guineas.

Today it would attract little attention but for the fact that it establishes a point of departure. It stands like an examination paper, marking the end of a course of studies, and it becomes a point of reference against which we can assess the later changes.

Something of Meldrum's tonal realism can be detected in the way the forms are modelled, but the dominating influence is undoubtedly that of Lambert. Even here, Dobell is more interested in what he knows about the forms than in what the eye tells him at any particular moment. Obscuring shadows are rifled of their secrets. He will not sacrifice what he knows to be true for what seems to be true under a specific effect of light. He will not pretend that he does not know what goes on simply because he cannot see it. If Meldrum could not see a form it did not exist for him. Past experience of the form counted for nothing. He would put down precisely what he saw, no more.

Dobell learnt from Lambert that the underlying structure was more important than the surface image and, although he was soon to discard every other aspect of Lambert's influence, he never rejected this point of view.

After the Matinée is undeniably a student's work. Its thin, dry paint echoes the late manner of Lambert. It finds acceptable solutions for conventional problems, but asks no questions that cannot be settled by resorting to classroom formulae. Everything about it is honest and conscientious, but it is also static and lifeless. His ballerinas are merely studio props as carefully posed as objects in a still-life.

18

CHAPTER TWO

The London Years: 1929–1938

For Dobell 1929 was to be a momentous year. His minor success in the Australian Art Quest was followed by a major success that was to reshape his life. He won the Society of Artists' Travelling Scholarship, which enabled him to study in England and on the Continent.

The painting that gained him this opportunity was a seated male nude. The model was posed in a corner of the studio, the head in shadows and inclined downwards at an angle to his left, his right arm bent above his shoulder, holding a drapery that he seems about to draw around himself. The modelling is almost photographic in its realism; the draughtsmanship is meticulous, and already there is evidence of that feeling for the tactile properties of paint that he was soon to explore as eagerly as any discoverer in a new world. The Scholarship was worth five hundred pounds.

It is safe to say that when Dobell sailed for England at the age of thirty he had not yet seen an original old master of any quality, or a significant original by a modern master.

This may not be of much consequence to the kind of painter who is prepared to start from scratch and who relies on the urgency of his vision to provide the means by which the vision can be realized. Nolan is such a painter; but Dobell is a traditionalist and his style could only grow to maturity after it had been fertilized by contact with the past.

Arriving in London in time to attend the Slade for the Winter term, he enrolled for the drawing classes of Henry Tonks and the painting classes of Wilson Steer. A little later on he received some private tuition from Sir William Orpen in a series of five or six visits.

In 1930 he won first prize for figure painting with the *Nude*

19

Ill. 3   *Study*, now in the Newcastle Art Gallery, and shared second prize for draughtsmanship with a young German student.

The year with Tonks, Steer and Orpen brought his formal art education to a close, but he continued to learn from the masters in the National Gallery especially from Rembrandt, Hals, Goya, Tintoretto, and El Greco.

In the summer of 1930 he visited Holland to study the Dutch masters. For three months he stayed at the home of Rient van Santen, a cousin of Van Gogh's, at The Hague. Together they studied in the Dutch museums and saw a huge retrospective exhibition of Van Goghs, borrowed from all over the world. This, too, made a terrific impact on Dobell. He saw in it a connection with Rembrandt, his first and deepest love. It was what he described as 'the heavy handed strength' in both masters that aroused his admiration.

Daumier drew his attention for similar reasons, but another aspect of his personality responded to the lightness and charm of Renoir. Later still he was to be stirred by the violence and passion of Soutine's portraits.

Ill. 8   A visit to Belgium in 1931, where he stayed a month in Bruges and did some painting, and to Paris, where he felt the full impact of Renoir, provided him with all the elements he needed for the formation of his own style.

It might be thought that an artist dressed in a patchwork of other men's styles could never be taken seriously, could never be thought of as anything but a kind of bower bird collecting shining scraps and eye-catching pieces.

But in reacting to each of these artists Dobell was fulfilling a part of himself. If he gathered a little here and something there, it was because his nature demanded it, and because it is common practice for all young artists to build their future on the groundwork of things they have borrowed from the past. What saved him from the shallows of eclecticism was the purpose for which the experiences were gathered.

As receptive as he was to the art of others, he was even more receptive to life itself. His overriding interest in humanity was

20

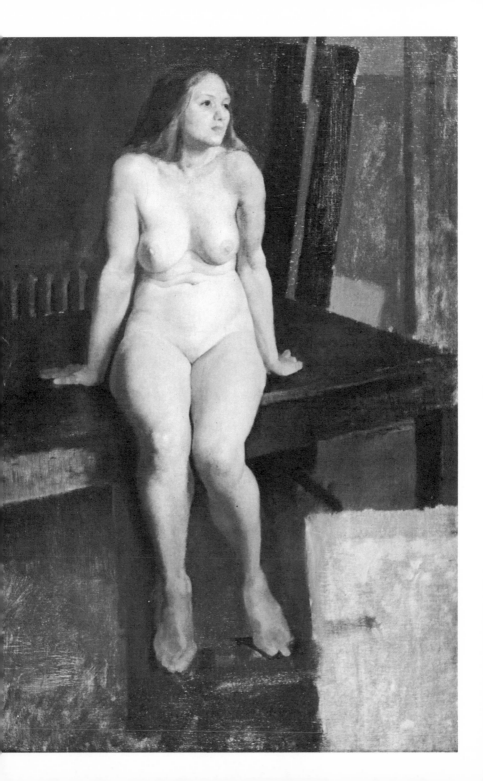

the factor that allowed him to absorb so much without suffering from aesthetic dyspepsia. All the various elements were broken down and assimilated by his passionate interest in people and their behaviour. He took only what he needed from the past in order to say what he felt and knew about life.

To borrow something simply because you happen to like it is one thing; to borrow something because that something is necessary to your growth as an individual is as blameless as a plant taking sustenance from the soil or sunlight.

Dobell needed Rembrandt and Renoir and all the others so that he could be himself. The borrowings did not block the emergence of a personal style, the personal style emerged because of the borrowings. All the separate pieces were fused together by the warmth of his desire to grasp life and hold it firmly, and when they had merged the result was something greater than the sum of all the parts.

During the first few years in London, Dobell began the process of fusing together these disparate stimuli in combinations that would liberate his own artistic personality.

Only at two intervals in his life has Dobell been a prolific painter. Sometimes the stream of creative energy almost seems to dry up, and in these lean years the works are few and far between. At other times the flood-gates open and the paintings pour like a deluge from his easel. The year 1936 was such a time, and though it was interrupted for about a year by his return to Sydney at the end of 1938, the spate continued until it was brought to an end by the court case in 1944. It was not until 1948 that Dobell was really back into his stride again and this second wave of creativity, stimulated by the landscape at Wangi and his two visits to New Guinea in 1949 and 1950, carried him through to the mid-fifties when his output was again interrupted by a long and serious illness.

From the first three years in London barely a dozen pictures have survived. All of them are small, the largest being the *Ill. 5* 1931 *Nude* which is $35\frac{1}{8} \times 27\frac{1}{8}$ in. They all assert his continuing allegiance to the conventions of naturalism. Marked distortions

22

of form for satirical emphasis or emotional purposes do not begin to appear before the middle of the decade.

The Slade prize-winning *Nude* and the portrait *London Boy* clearly show the impact the Slade has had upon the groundwork he acquired from Lambert and the Julian Ashton School. Although the forms are still firmly and meticulously modelled and the contours are emphatically stressed, the handling has gained in fluency and his observation has increased in subtlety. *Ills. 3, 4*

However, one has only to compare the Slade *Nude* and the 1931 *Nude* to see what a difference a year made to his painting. He was learning rapidly. There is nothing of the student in the *Ills. 3, 5*

4
London Boy,
1930

5 *Nude, 1931*

later *Nude*. He has learnt that it is not necessary to state everything you know about a form in order to be convincing. He has allowed the shadows to encroach naturally about the figure, like a tide of darkness lapping about the lightest areas. The figure looms from the background like one of Michelangelo's captive slaves half freed from its marble block.

The paint itself has a Watteauesque delicacy and the rhythms of the pose could have been suggested by Watteau's *La Toilette* in the Wallace Collection.

Yet it is Rembrandt that is most clearly called to mind by its use of tone, though the pose itself is perhaps too consciously elegant to have appealed to Rembrandt's robust sense of reality. The figure has been carefully arranged to make the most of its flowing curves. It is no longer a study designed to gain and express knowledge; it is a picture in which the nude is used for its picturesque properties alone; as a surface that reflects light, and as a vehicle for the expression of a rhythmic sense.

Curiously enough, the male counterpart of this nude was not painted until 1939. The *Boy Bathing* bears within its style   *Ill. 6*

6 Boy Bathing, 1939

the evidence of eight years added experience, but its aim is identical with that of the 1931 *Nude*. It was, in fact, painted from a London sketch of this period. Dobell shared a studio with another Australian painter, John Passmore, and to save money on models they would pose for each other. The *Boy Bathing* was painted from a drawing he made of Passmore at that time.

Later still in the paintings of New Guinea natives it is the rhythmic element that dominates. The figures are drawn in with vigorously rhythmical lines and the modelling is often only hinted at by touches of paint to suggest a highlight or a shadow.

However, the nude never attracts Dobell's interest as strongly as the face. There is only one category of art in which he shows less interest and that is still-life.

Although in these early years his approach to portraiture is hesitant and intermittent, it becomes, with maturity, an absorbing passion that leads him to the creation of his finest works of art. In these first few years there are relatively few portraits – he seemed more interested in landscape and genre.

London stirred his imagination. Its parks and streets, the river and its bridges and, above all, the Londoners themselves provided him with an inexhaustible source of material.

Three portraits were painted between 1931 and 1932, and they give us an idea of Dobell's starting-point as a portraitist. Two are self-portraits and the third is a profile study of a young boy called *Billy Frost*.

Dobell did not share Rembrandt's fascination with the self-portrait and in later years he has never returned to it, but in those lean days of the Depression he found in himself a model he was not obliged to pay for his services. Consequently there *Ill. 7* are a number of self-portraits of which the 1931 version is reproduced.

All three are marked by an intensity of observation that shows the artist's determination to put in all the facts. They are all carefully modelled, the light areas being built up by successive layers of paint applied in strokes that follow the contours of

26

the form as in a drawing, the darker tones being applied more thinly though never quite transparently.

This drawing-like character of his paint is a characteristic that Dobell rarely abandons for long, though the way in which he draws with paint changes as his confidence is increased by experience.

Of the three, the *Billy Frost* is probably the most accomplished from the stylistic point of view. The profile is defined with knife-edged precision, but the tendency towards a bas-relief effect is offset by the play of brush strokes that sets up a subtle internal rhythm of its own, and one that sometimes runs across and against the containing lines of the contour, like water playing on a statue.

This kind of resolution of the problems inherent in profile portraiture could only be arrived at by an artist of the most acute sensitivity.

None of the landscapes of the period quite reach this level although *St Paul's from Waterloo Bridge* (1931) is, to say the least of it, a satisfying exercise in Impressionism. It, too, is hatched in with repeated brush strokes in a style that is derived from drawing techniques, though it is possible to find a faint echo of Van Gogh in the animation of its surface.

He sometimes painted landscapes *en plein air*, but he preferred to work from sketches in his studio. *Old Houses, Bruges* and *Ill. 8* *Canal, Bruges* were actually painted on the spot. The former is a rather conventional painting, a little dated in its attitude to the picturesque but full of painterly qualities that indicate a maturing talent of some stature; the latter is probably the most charming of his early impressionistic landscapes. Painted with *Ill. 9* much less vehemence than the London river scene, it creates a mood of tranquillity that he was to repeat in a number of paintings about this time.

All that was best in Dobell's early manner comes out in a *Ill. 27* genre painting of 1932 called *Boy at the Basin*. It was accepted and hung in the 'Gem Room' of the Royal Academy Exhibition of 1933. P. Konody, the art critic for the *Observer*, praised it

28

8 Canal, Bruges, 1931

without mentioning Dobell's name. In writing of a certain painter's work he went on to say 'but a far better picture in the same style is *Boy at the Basin* . . .' thus creating the impression that it was another work by the same painter.

Small in scale, reticent in colour, and intimate in character, it was hardly the sort of painting to attract attention to itself. Nothing about it clamoured for recognition. One could easily pass it by with a casual glance. If it was a 'gem' it was no flashing diamond, furnace-hearted ruby, or harlequin opal. It had the serene withdrawn delicacy of a moonstone. Everything was understated and in a minor key. Later on Dobell learnt to trumpet his statements in a major key (the ill-starred *Joshua* *Smith* is a brilliant example) but many of his finest things have been said *sotto voce*.

Ill. 75

Without comparing him to those past masters of the gentle art of ineloquence, Piero della Francesca and Vermeer, there is something in the silvery tonality of the painting that stirs up memories of Piero, and something in the tranquil inevitability of the composition and in the way the light binds form to form that sets the mind thinking of Vermeer.

Boy at the Basin is probably his most impersonal painting, if we use the word 'impersonal' to mean that he has subdued those qualities of style that make one think of the artist rather than the picture. It is as though he had deliberately chosen to write in copperplate because his natural handwriting imposed too personal a bias. Paradoxically, in painting himself out of the picture he has revealed himself more clearly than ever. Under certain circumstances deliberate ineloquence can tell us more than we can learn from would-be eloquence.

This is not a picture in which to study Dobell's style, but it is a picture that takes us close to the quiet mainspring of Dobell's art. It is a simple subject – the sort of action we would be likely to see as an unremarkable and recurring part of our daily lives, and which only becomes memorable because Dobell has been able to isolate a moment of unmemorable time by trapping it in a work of art.

This is his secret. He sees the ordinary and paints it as though it was extraordinary; he sees the commonplace and paints it as though it was unique; he sees the ugly and paints it as though it was beautiful. It is a characteristic he shares with Rembrandt.

After finishing the *Boy at the Basin* Dobell thought to return for another term at the Slade. With that idea in mind he painted a picture which has come to be known as the *Summer Composition Slade School*. He planned to submit it as a summer project. It depicts a flat shelf on a rocky cliff. A youth with a towel over his head is sunbathing on the ledge. Another figure climbs from below, like one of the bathers summoned from

30

9 *A Bridge in London, 1930*

the river by the Battle of Cascina in the copies of Michelangelo's lost cartoon. Still another figure stands drying his hair,
and this figure is taken directly from the sketch he made in his
studio for the *Boy at the Basin*. Though painted with the same
finesse it is not an entirely satisfactory picture. Our interest is
too evenly divided between the rocks and the figures. We can
admire the skill with which he uses shadows to tie the forms
together; we are fascinated by a design that is as bold as that
of any abstract and by the subtle precision of the figure painting, but the picture as a whole lacks unity. In any case it was
never submitted at the Slade. Dobell went back to school for

a week but found the atmosphere cramping and uncongenial, his new teachers incapable of teaching him the things he wanted to know.

Up till this time most of Dobell's paintings had been deliberate and carefully composed studies, although the brisk and spontaneous *Onion Seller* of 1931 pointed the way towards greater freedom.

Ill. 10

After the *Boy at the Basin* his confidence increased. He left the studio and began to find his subjects in the parks, streets, and cafés of the city. If he found a face, a gesture, or a situation that attracted him he would pin-point the essentials in quick and surreptitious sketches. It embarrassed him to be caught sketching in this way, so he would take great pains to disguise his activity. Later, in his studio, he would work from these notes, but the finished paintings preserved the directness and spontaneity of the sketches. The paint was applied with less concern for incidental details. Broad forms were summarized in the simplest manner and essential details were written in with the brevity of shorthand. After all, he was really working from memory, aided only by the jottings he had made on the spot. The model was no longer in front of him. He could not fill out the statement with circumstantial details even if he wanted to. As in all memories of an experience much is forgotten or blurred. Only the essentials are retained.

Curiously enough, this is the method Dobell continued to use for most of his portraiture. He sharpens his observations by sketching the model from various angles, and then constructs the final portrait from the knowledge he has gained through these exercises.

Woman in Café and *Consuelita* were painted within a few months of one another in 1933, yet they are totally unalike. If the *Onion Seller* looked forward to a later freedom, *Consuelita* looks back to a strictness that was soon to disappear for ever. Artistically speaking *Consuelita* is a sister to *Billy Frost*. It is painted with the same precise outlines – outlines that are as severe and unequivocal as a wire fence. The forms are vigorously

32

10 Onion Seller, 1931

contained yet they have an amplitude that is not apparent in the earlier portrait. Again one is reminded of sculpture, and again the brush strokes flow over the static forms like water. It represents Dobell's last attempt to achieve simplicity by schematically monumentalizing the sitter. In future he will trust his intuition and his memory to select only what is necessary.

Although *Woman in Café* marks a stylistic starting-point it has qualities that are soon to be submerged and which will only reappear spasmodically in his later work. In the following year

Ill. 11

33

(1934) Dobell painted a similar subject in his *Woman in* Ill. 12 *Restaurant* and a comparison between the two shows the extent of the change.

The woman in the earlier picture is observed with great sympathy. She leans forward comfortably. There is a cup of tea on the table and she rests her head against her right hand. There is a sense of slight fatigue in the pose, as though she had spent the afternoon shopping and is glad of a chance to sit down, or perhaps she had been to a matinée and is only thinking of something she had seen in the play. The whole painting is uncomplicated, generous, and warm. It records a moment of singular unimportance, but the sympathy implicit in the artist's treatment lifts the picture and makes it memorable.

The woman of the second picture does not receive such gentle treatment. She, too, leans forward on the table to light a

11 Woman in Café, 1933

12 *Woman in Restaurant, 1934*

13 Sketch for The Speakers, Hyde Park, 1934

cigarette, but the heavily swelling lines and accentuated bulk of
the figure create an image of over-indulgence that could stand
as a symbol for the sin of gluttony. Yet even here he does not
condemn, he merely observes and comments. One has only
to visualize the way Ensor, Nolde, or Grosz would have treated
such a subject to realize the extent of his restraint. He is not
above making a caustic comment when he feels it is called for,
but he has not the reformer's zeal to pressure him into a gush
of bitter denunciations.

Nevertheless, *Woman in Restaurant* is the first of a series of
satirical paintings that occupy an important place in his *œuvre*.
Within a year or so such acidulous studies will become the rule
and gentler paintings the exception. Landscapes will still be

36

plotted with a kinder eye; the pleasure he takes in parks and streets will not be quite so alloyed by his sense of the ridiculous, though even now the parks are filling up with talkers and staring faces that jolt him out of his tranquil detachment. A growing disquiet obliges him to look more closely at the floating world, at the street with its freight of faces, at the faces with their jealously guarded secrets shouted in every line.

Five hundred pounds does not last for ever, and these were the years of a grim depression. Jobs were scarce and eagerly sought. An unknown artist, however talented, could hardly hope to live by his painting alone. Despite the most stringent economies Dobell's slender bank account continued to waste away. Poverty brought him to the dingiest bed-sitting rooms

14 *The Speakers, Hyde Park, 1934*

of Pimlico and Bayswater. At one stage he had so little money that he had to share a room with a professional burglar. As it happened the arrangement proved quite satisfactory. While the burglar was out at night working at his trade, Dobell slept in the only bed. In the day-time while Dobell was at the art school learning his trade, the burglar enjoyed his repose.

Sometimes he was lucky. When the New Zealand artist, Fred Coventry, went to Egypt to do some work for the Orient

15 *The Dirt Cart, 1936*

16 *Maid at the Window, 1937*

Line he let Dobell have his studio, which looked down on to
the main street of Bayswater. From these windows he made
sketches that grew into some of his most delightful paintings –
The Dust Cart, *The Dirt Cart*, *The Baker's Cart*, and the charming   *Ill. 15*
The Little Milliner. Even when Coventry came back from   *Ill. 17*
Egypt he still continued to live there for a while. The two
artists would amuse themselves while drawing the floating
world below them by guessing what the people were talking
about. Dobell still has a sketch of two very badly dressed women
saying, according to him: 'But she supports herself so badly.'

39

17 The Little Milliner, 1936

At other times he shared with other equally impoverished Australian artists, and he earned money wherever he could, by the occasional sale of a picture for a few guineas, by working as a commercial artist, as an illustrator for cheap magazines, or as a film extra.

Things took a brighter turn in 1936 when Arthur Murch landed the job of decorating the Wool Pavilion for the Glasgow Fair of 1937. Murch gathered round him a group of fourteen Australian artists then living in London – Dobell, Wallace Thornton, George Duncan, Alison Rehfisch, Jean Appleton, James and Ruth Cook were included – and they were all paid ten pounds a week for six months. This was the most affluent period of the nine years Dobell spent in England.

18 Costume Study, 1935

19 *Tired Nippy, 1937*

20 *Boy Lounging, 1937*

Gifted with a rare and sparkling sense of humour that prevents him from indulging in the luxuries of self-pity he is none the less endowed with a sensitivity so acute that it almost wrecked his career on a number of occasions. Paradoxically it is from this sensitivity that he draws the perceptions and intuitions that make his portraits so revealing. A mind less subtly attuned to others would never command the insight necessary to great portraiture, though a tougher mind would be safer from the wounds such insight must invariably inflict.

Contrary to the normal course by which our sensitivities gradually harden and become calloused by the rub of experience, Dobell has never acquired a thick protective skin. On the contrary, he seems to have gradually lost his earlier resilience.

21 *Sketch for Irish Youth, 1935*

22 *Sketch for Irish Youth, 1938*

23 *Irish Youth, 1938*

24 The Charlady, 1936

The years between 1935 and 1938 were vintage years for Dobell, the artist, because he was able to protect himself with the swordplay of satire. Experience gave his work an added pungency. As he saw more and more deeply into the world about him he used satire to keep the sight from reaching a mortal part. It was as protective as a moat to a castle or a quill to a porcupine.

Even so, he rarely felt the need to give his satire too sharp a point. In all but two or three cases he observes the ridiculous with a clear but tolerant eye. In *Toilette* for instance he paints *Ill. 28* a bulky nude with ruthless honesty, but the mood is one of earthy vigour rather than criticism or satire.

Pretentiousness seems to have been his main target, for it, of all the vices and frailties, called forth his most stringent rebukes.

In 1936 he painted *The Duchess Disrobes* from a gouache sketch inspired by the pompous antics of a penguin in the London Zoo. Something in the stumpy, flapping ungainliness of the bird's movements conjured up an image of a *grande dame* about to bathe. In the sketch we can still see the penguin origins of the figure. The large flipper-like feet, the awkward stance, and the robe falling from her arm like a wing, all indicate the source of its inspiration. In the final version the bird analogy has been lost. The figure has taken on a mock elegance. The heavy body balances precariously on improbably slender legs. He has taken great delight in showing us a figure of dignity in its least dignified state. Dressed in the robes and regalia of her position, the Duchess would undoubtedly be an imposing figure. Here she is shown in all the weakness of her ageing flesh. It is a ruthless exposure, and somehow one feels a little sorry for the lady caught so completely off guard.

No doubt Dobell intended us to feel the subtle pathos hidden in the ridiculous image, but there is no ambiguity in his attitude to *Mrs South Kensington*. It is an extraordinary portrait *Ill. 25* of a dried-up spirit. With masterly brevity he has recorded the narrowed eyes, the grey wrinkled skin, the bitter mouth, and the carefully fashionable hat in a little masterpiece of ice-cold observation. It is a face animated solely by animosity, a malevolent life-denying mask for a dead soul.

One of the astonishing things about Dobell's portraiture is his ability to adjust his style to the nature of the personality he is portraying. It is evident here and it becomes much more evident during the next twenty years. If the character of his sitter is broad and generous, he paints broadly and generously. If the character is contained and inward looking, he uses brush strokes that convey this fact. In his later portraits one has only to look at a few square inches of a painted sleeve to know what sort of person is wearing it.

It is the same with *Mrs South Kensington*. The paint is dry and stringy. The colour is bleached and dusty. He has painted the features with hurried little strokes as though the face had been modelled by tiny claws scratching it into shape. There is a downward draw of claw marks along the nose, the same rhythm is repeated in the cheeks, and again in the piled-up hair. Elsewhere the face breaks into little eddies and flurries of paint that are repeated in the fur round her neck and in the flowers on her hat.

Dobell never again painted a portrait with such venom. He never again chose a subject in which the spark of life was so nearly smothered by a deliberate rejection of its warmth. Many subsequent works take note of the absurd, the extreme, and the off-beat, but Dobell's art lies too close to the centre of everyday existence for these excursions to the periphery to be anything but occasional pieces.

Ill. 24 *The Charlady* is a revealing complement to *Mrs South Kensington*. A sympathetic obverse to the latter's unpleasant reverse. Handled with even greater brevity and economy of means, it is infused with a clear-sighted generosity. Nothing is glossed over or minimized. Much of the drawing is simply scratched into the wet paint with the handle of a brush, but all the wispy tiredness and frailty has been accurately noted and set down. Once again, the way in which it is actually painted adds to our understanding of the character.

48

25 *Mrs South Kensington, 1937*

Whether by instinct or conscious intention, Dobell has selected from his armoury of styles the pictorial weapons best equipped to expose the inner realities of his subject. The scratches that define the forms not only suggest wispy fragility, they also have a wiry strength about them, a springy resilience that implies an ability to cope with life. *The Charlady*, though physically frail, has resources of strength that have long since vanished for *Mrs South Kensington*.

It seems as though the artist had become obsessed with states of exhaustion at this time. *Tired Nippy*, *The Sleeping Greek*, and *The Dead Landlord* are all concerned with exhaustion of one kind or another.

Ills. 19, 30, 29

The nippy, who rests between calls, was tired out by under-nourishment before the day began and now, foundering in a sea of weariness, she slumps for a moment of uneaseful rest, for she knows that at any moment a bell will ring or a voice will call, and she will have to make the infinite effort to answer it.

The Greek sleeps easily and peacefully for he is still young and as he is a waiter in a restaurant in Bayswater Road he does not lack food. But the hours are long and the pay inadequate, especially since he must send money home to his family in Cyprus. His name is Aegus Gabriell Ides and because Dobell sometimes dines in the restaurant they have struck up an acquaintanceship, and in his hours off duty he sometimes comes and poses for the artist. On another occasion Dobell made a pen-and-wash drawing of him and a sketch in oils, and four years later when he had returned to Sydney he painted *The Cypriot* from it.

Ill. 26
Ill. 63

The latent energy of the sleeper is brilliantly conveyed to us through the dynamics of the composition. By placing the head diagonally and by looking at it from above, Dobell sets up a system of movements and counter-movements that might at first seem inappropriate for such a subject, however natural the pose appears to be. Yet it is precisely this quality that makes the head so memorable. Though we are denied the expressiveness of the eyes, though the personality is withdrawn and the features

26 *Sketch for The Cypriot, 1937*

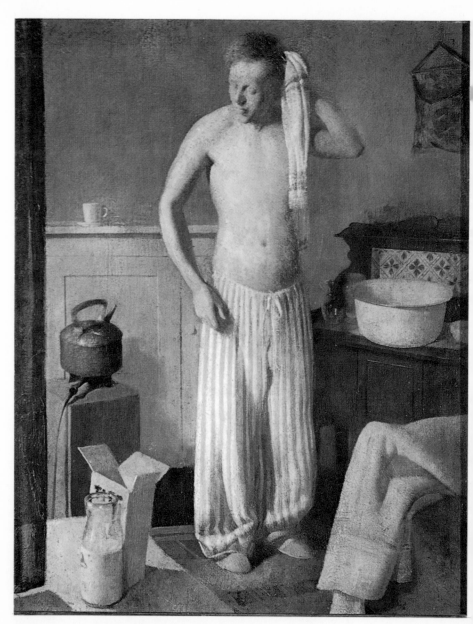

27 Boy at the Basin, 1932

28 *Toilette, 1936*

are made uncommunicative by sleep, the artist still manages to convey to us a sense of dormant vitality.

The warm artificial light falls softly on the forehead, loses strength as the head sinks on to the chest between hunched shoulders, then catches the peaks of a white collar that holds the face like a calyx. In passing it glances along the ridge of the nose and collects on the high cheek-bones. Ridges in the textured paint follow the swell and recession of forms so that one is reminded of a carving before the final polish removes all evidence of the chisel's work.

At the time he painted *The Sleeping Greek* Dobell was living in a room in a house in Bayswater owned by a cabinet-maker and his wife. One morning he was aroused by his frantic landlady and hustled down to the basement where she lived with her husband amid an indescribable confusion of second-hand furniture in various stages of rehabilitation.

The landlord was dead on the floor. He had fallen from a chair and was too heavy for the woman to lift on to the large double bed he had so recently vacated. Dobell had never seen a dead body before. He had to steel himself to touch the still warm corpse, but eventually the two of them hoisted him on to the bed and proceeded to lay him out. When this was done the woman went to the dressing-table and began to brush her hair with dazed monotonous regularity, staring at herself in the mirror but seeing nothing. As Dobell watched the scene in horrified fascination, the woman announced that he was to have a ham funeral (no one in the street had ever been given a ham funeral before) and the artist was sent to fetch the relatives.

When he returned to his room he could not shake the image of the dead landlord from his mind. He immediately began to shape it on to paper and from the sketch he developed his most striking and bizarre genre painting.

Years later Patrick White was to take this painting as the starting-point for his brilliant and imaginative play *The Ham Funeral*. In the foreword to the programme he wrote: 'During a visit to my native country in 1946 I met William Dobell, who told me how he came to paint *The Dead Landlord*, and suggested the incident might contain the theme for a play. Early the following year I returned to London to gather up my goods and chattels after deciding finally to settle in Australia. I was the only lodger in a house in Ebury Street, where I had lived on going to London as a young man, to which I had returned on and off during the nineteen-thirties, and where I experienced the first months of the London blitz in the basement and coal cellar under the pavement. By 1947 there was a bomb site next door. Blast and the lean years had stripped the house of most of its superfluities.

'As I sat in my empty room I began to play with Dobell's anecdote of how his landlord had died, how the landlady had taken down her hair, announcing there would be a ham funeral and that he must go to fetch the relatives.

'Out of those original facts and my own self-searchings and experiences as a young man in the house in Ebury Street the play of *The Ham Funeral* developed.'

The Dead Landlord is a strange and disturbing painting. The *Ill. 29* light flickers through the gloom without rhyme or reason. In fact, the source of light seems to be the inert body itself. It glows in the foreground with a livid phosphorescence, like a great pale fish stranded on a double bed. Beyond in the shadows the distrait widow brushes her hair mechanically.

Despite the emotional disturbance following in the wake of the experience, the artist rejected any impulse to abandon himself to the mood of the moment and to fashion the picture from the flaring sensations it had touched off in him. Although he was attracted by the expressionistic elements in the art of Van Gogh and Soutine he was not prepared to emulate their total surrender to the subjective approach.

We learn to expect the unexpected in his art. When he painted *The Sleeping Greek* he used every device of dynamic composition *Ill. 30* for a subject that would normally suggest a more static groundwork. The effect was to take us behind the passive façade and indicate the true nature of the sleeper.

29 *The Dead Landlord, 1936*

Here, where one would expect the composition to take its character from the turbulent emotional currents of its theme, Dobell has deliberately chosen to relate the tragi-comedy in terms of almost mathematical formality. By deliberately distorting the perspective of the bedhead and making it continue the horizontal line of the mantelpiece he has created an insistent horizontal at the point indicated by the golden mean. Similarly the woman's back curves along the longitudinal division of the same proportion.

The picture rings with clear echoes. The curving rail at the foot of the bed repeats the curve of the mirror above the fireplace. With a touch of strange humour the sprightly bow of the

56

30 The Sleeping Greek, 1936

31 *The Red Lady, 1937*

pyjama cord, perched like an insect on the dead man's stomach, mocks the formal tidiness of carved gilt bows on top of the mirror. The lines of the pillow ape the woman's curving buttocks. Even the clock on the mantelpiece and the bedhead are first cousins. Everything is precisely calculated and placed according to a classic formula. He uses tight reins to hold the mood in check. By extraordinary insight amounting almost to an identification with the woman's state of mind, he has felt

58

hat only the strictest controls could prevent a collapse into hysteria. How clearly the composition indicates the woman's feelings! Its artificial formality is a pictorial counterpart of the instinct that urges the woman to brush her hair. They both represent a desperately forced attempt to hold on to normalcy in a situation that could so easily get out of hand.

No doubt there are many who share Dobell's sensitivity to other people's feelings, but what makes Dobell so rare an artist is his unerring skill in projecting that insight in pictorial terms.

Sometimes it involves taking a course that artists less gifted than he might regard as wrong-headed or even fatal to its purpose. Few would have thought so rigid an armature could be suitable for the theme of *The Dead Landlord*, yet the artist justified his decision by using it as a key to unlock and expose the deepest psychological truths about the woman's condition.

Three other works of this period give us an idea of the variety of approaches the artist is able to use. The *Irish Youth* indicates *Ill. 23* a line of development that will, within a few years, bring us to the portrait of Joshua Smith. Distortion is used discreetly, and only if its use will tell us something of the sitter's personality that a more photographic likeness would not reveal. Exaggerations arise out of the desire to discover the essentials.

The portraitist must have the courage to deny the evidence of his eye and to give credence to the hinting of his instinct. And courage is needed, for, at those times when the information provided by the eye is at variance with that arising from our instincts, it is much easier to believe the visible evidence. Delicate judgements are required, for the portrait painter is bound by honour to alter the visual appearance of his sitter only if the alteration reveals the character more clearly, or in a truer way. Distortion for its own sake is not for the painter of portraits. It belongs to the decorator, and for him it is not dishonest.

Again and again, in portraits and genre, Dobell recalls the methods of Dickens, though the sentiment has been replaced by greater impartiality and the humour is somewhat more caustic.

They share a common interest in all the many types of men and women and in the incidents that befall them. The pen and the brush probe deeply and draw forth the natures of those under examination. Often a little exaggeration is necessary here or there to point an idiosyncrasy, or it may be found necessary to refocus the attention on a detail in order to evoke a hidden characteristic. So the finished portrait becomes a quintessence from which all unessentials have been eliminated.

Neither *Miss Tatty* nor *The Red Lady* are real portraits; they are studies of types – generalizations that have the impact of portraits because we know such characters exist. We are not asked to think of them as individuals, but to accept them as symbols.

Miss Tatty is all the primly dressed, short-sighted, benign but
Ill. 31   slightly vacuous old ladies one has ever met. *The Red Lady* is the fat woman of any circus. Both were painted because Dobell cannot resist the extreme form of any human characteristic, but unlike Leonardo, who prowled the streets with his sketch-book in search of radical variants from the facial norm, Dobell only responds to faces and figures if they epitomize a common trait or tendency. He has absolutely no interest in real abnormality or deformity. There is nothing wrong with *The Red Lady* except that she is extremely fat. She is red only because she is fat and it is a very hot day.

Side by side with these character studies, portraits, and genre paintings, the artist continued to record the life of the streets and parks. There are no figures at all in some of them, and in others the figures are purely incidental. Among the trees in
Ill. 34   *Kensington Gardens*, *Regent's Park*, and *London Zoo* he learnt the landscape techniques that were to reach their fullest expression at Wangi more than a decade later.

Sometimes the streets are empty. There is no sign of life in the *Street in Royal Oak*. A few idlers enjoy the soft sunlight of *Park Lane*; *Alexander Street* is deserted except for two small children; a small group stands in the rain waiting for a bus
Ill. 33   outside *The White Horse Inn, Dorking* and two bicyclists have

32 Cockney Mother, 1937

Ill. 35 just passed a fruit cart in a *Street in Pimlico*. From an upstairs
window he made three delightful studies of carts and patient
Ill. 15 horses – *The Dust Cart*, *The Dirt Cart*, and *The Baker's Cart* –
and once in 1936 he went back to the river and made a painting
Ill. 36 of the piers and spans of a temporary bridge.

But it was the life in the streets that really fascinated him. In
the West End he sees an over-dressed dowager clutching a
pekinese as she waits impatiently for her car. He paints *My Lady*
Ill. 38 *Waits* with a fluffy agitation of brush strokes that mimics my
lady's feathery irritation to perfection.

With breath-taking economy he catches the professional
Ill. 17 elegance of *The Little Milliner* making her determined way
through the thickening fog. The outlines of her dark cape and
skirt have an eccentricity that Conder would have admired,

33 *The White Horse Inn, Dorking, 1935*

34 Kensington Gardens, 1935

and the finely judged distribution of space would have appealed to the artists of the Ukiyo-e.

One of the finest of his London paintings is the haunting *Street Singer* of 1938. There are critics who claim that Dobell never surpassed this painting in warmth of feeling or power of expression. Perhaps they are right. Later works may have greater brilliance and some may reveal a more astonishing insight, but none are more deeply touched with unsentimental sympathy or stated with such uncomplicated directness.

Like so many of his London pictures it was painted from a window looking down on the subject. Perhaps the security of

Ill. 37

63

35 Street in Pimlico, 1937

36 A London Bridge, 1936

being able to observe without being observed had a stimulating effect on him. Safe from the possibility of embarrassment by being caught in the act he could work in greater freedom.

In 1962 a copy of his painting by another hand was found in the storerooms of the Art Gallery of New South Wales. Whether it was intended as a deliberate forgery, or as an innocent exercise such as students make during their course of studies, is not a matter that need concern us here.

What emerged from a study of the two paintings before the copy was destroyed was the way weaknesses in the copy pinpointed excellences in the original. They showed up felicities that one could so easily take for granted because they seemed

65

37 Street Singer, 1938

to be achieved without effort. In the copy, the thumb of the left hand was a mere squiggle of paint; the original also seemed to have been painted in a single brisk gesture of the brush, but one felt the presence of bones beneath the surface. Varying pressures had spread the paint with an instinctive feeling for the form it was describing. Pressure thinned the paint over the knuckle, making it taut as skin is taut when the bone lies close to the surface. Then the pressure relaxed and the paint fattened out over the fleshy parts of the thumb. In the copy the back of the skirt formed a straight line. In the original it is also a straight line and yet, by almost imperceptible variations in pressure, we were made aware of the bulk of the hip beneath the skirt. So, also, in a dozen different details the copy failed and in failing pointed to the subtle perfection of the original.

66

38 My Lady Waits, 1937

But, however much we might admire the means by which Dobell accomplishes his purpose, in the long run it is the purpose itself that interests us.

Drawn to the window by the sound of music he has looked down into the dusk-dim street and seen a stocky woman playing a guitar and singing as she plays. The woman has the compact strength of a Brueghel peasant. One cannot believe that she would sing with any skill or elegance. Perhaps it is a country song she sings, or a popular ballad. Her clothes have a countrified simplicity about them. Her voice would be strong, sweet perhaps, but untrained. Yet she plays the guitar. Perhaps she may even have a musical background of some sort – a failed opera-singer down on her luck, or a teacher who could find no pupils.

39 *Woman Watching a Funeral, 1938*

Whoever she was, whatever she sang, whether well or badly, it touched a responsive chord in the artist at the window. With the sort of chalks children use at school he drew the figure on to a sheet of poor quality drawing paper, and later painted the picture from it. That one moment of time when the song in the street and the artist's sensibilities were mingled together has been recorded and the moment has become timeless.

Other figures in other streets have caught his imagination and guided his brush. Down in the East End he comes across a *Ill. 32* slippered *Cockney Mother*, shabby, shapeless and unkempt, holding in her arms a warmly bundled baby in a yellow bonnet.

Ill. 39 He sees a *Woman Watching a Funeral* from the vantage point of her front window. She is heavy and phlegmatic, full of

68

40 *Woman in a Hamburger, 1944*

41
Cockney Kid with Hoop,
1936

interest but emotionally unaffected by the event she watches. She has even spread a rug over the window-sill so she can lean her elbows on it with greater comfort. The face and pose are closely observed but briefly stated, and an extremely static composition creates an appropriate sense of inevitability. From another window – in a more affluent part of the city – a uniformed maid peers into the street from between lace curtains.

Back in the East End he sees a bold young hussy of a girl with *Ill. 41* a hoop standing with her hands on her hips, as she must have seen her mother stand a hundred times.

Often he would watch the costermongers in their pearly finery, shaking their ostrich plumes as they dance to the music of an accordion. He followed them to Epsom Downs on Derby Day and sketched their roistering enjoyment with the gusto of a Rowlandson and the atmospheric delicacy of a Renoir.

In Hyde Park in 1937 he made an oil sketch of a high-spirited party playing a rough and tumble game of saddle-my-nag. *Ill. 42*

Many of these subjects haunted his imagination for years and resulted in paintings made half a world away from the sites and sights that inspired them.

Towards the end of 1938, Dobell returned to Sydney. The Munich crisis convinced him that Europe would soon be at war, but the immediate cause of his return was news of his father's failing health – he was to die soon after his son's return. Dobell never intended to settle in England. During his nine years residence in London he made no real effort to establish himself as an artist. He exhibited only three pictures – *Boy at* *Ill. 27* *the Basin* at the Royal Academy (1933), *Maid at the Window* at *Ill. 16* the New English Art Club (1937), and *Street Singer* with the *Ill. 37* London Group (1938) – none of which were sold. When he arrived in Sydney his cases contained almost all the paintings and drawings he had made in Europe. Now nearing forty he was still unknown, except to a circle of friends. Soon that was to change and within five years he became the most talked about artist Australia has ever produced.

71

42 *Sketch for Saddle-My-Nag, 1937*

43 *Saddle-My-Nag, 1941*

CHAPTER THREE

The Sydney Years: 1938–1944

The Sydney Dobell returned to was very different to the one he left. The whole climate of artistic opinion was beginning to change. On 13 July 1938 a group of forward-looking artists had met together in Melbourne to found the Contemporary Art Society. Modern art was about to find a voice.

During the 1930s interest in the new movements had gradually quickened, and each year from 1933 onwards the Australian public had the opportunity of seeing loan exhibitions of paintings by some of Europe's contemporary masters.

While Dobell was still in England, the Australian art critic, Basil Burdett, was at work selecting paintings for the first really comprehensive collection of modern French and British art to be shown in Australia. Sponsored by Sir Keith Murdoch, Managing Director of the Melbourne *Herald*, it was shown in Australia on the eve of the Second World War.

Today the list of paintings reads like the catalogue of a major museum of modern art, and the effect on Australia's growing awareness of the modern schools was incalculable. There were nine Picassos, eight paintings each by Matisse and Van Gogh, seven each by Cézanne and Gauguin, five by Rouault, four by Braque, two by Modigliani, and individual paintings by Bonnard, Chagall, Chirico, Dali, Derain, Dufy, Ernst, Friesz, Gris, Laurencin, Léger, Lurçat, Marquet, Nicholson, Seurat, Signac, Soutine, Sutherland, Toulouse-Lautrec, Utrillo, Valadon, van Dongen, Vlaminck, Vuillard, Wadsworth, and Wood.

Many young artists who had not yet been to Europe now had the opportunity of studying at first-hand some of the masterpieces that had established the character of modern painting.

To many it came as a confirmation of previously formed attitudes; to some it came as a revelation that was to redirect their creative energies; to the conservatives it was final and convincing proof that art had slipped into anarchy or insanity; to the general public it was a proclamation that a basic revolution had taken place, that many of the old values had perished and that art, and the world, must be looked at from a radically new angle.

Nearly two generations of Europeans had grown up in the awareness of these changes, but the modern movement burst on many Australians with the suddenness of an explosion. They were presented with a *fait accompli* which required a convulsive readjustment of aesthetic values. Naturally there were those who could not, or would not, make these adjustments and ironically, the artist who suffered most in the ensuing clash between the two opposing groups was William Dobell, who belonged neither to the one, nor the other.

Such was the turbulent artistic atmosphere the artist found on his return.

His first months were spent securing a place to live, setting up a studio, and finding a job. For the first six months he stayed with one of his sisters, but on 25 May 1939 he started part-time teaching at the East Sydney Technical College, and shortly after this he found an apartment overlooking the busiest part of Sydney's cosmopolitan King's Cross. At first he taught for only four hours a week, but this was increased to six hours, then to ten, and finally in 1940 to twelve hours a week. At the end of the first term in 1941 he gave up his job as a teacher and was set to work painting camouflage at various aerodromes. Later on he became a war artist for the Civil Construction Corps, and painted the memorable series of pictures now in the Australian War Memorial Museum at Canberra.

London left a powerful impression on him – indeed so strong was its influence that it took the artist two or three years before he could see Sydney as it really was. The first years were largely spent in painting pictures based on London sketches, and

4 Nude Study, 1940

although his style was beginning to change once again, the changes reflected a deepening awareness of European tradition and took little account of the local scene. London provided the subject-matter and Renoir the stylistic starting-point.

Perhaps the most significant and obvious change occured in his use of colour. By and large, the pictures actually painted in London are distinguished by their subtle use of a restricted colour range.

45 Study of a Youth Seated, 1941

Whether it was the influence of Renoir, the stronger light of Australia, or both working together, his palette became more vivid and luminous after 1939. Even his London subjects began to sparkle with an intoxicating freedom. Blues and greens form shimmering backgrounds of shot silk. Figures begin to lose their edges, they almost dissolve in the peacock light, though he fixes their weight and volume in a play of broad, dense shadows. He will never allow them to slip out of their bodies to become as air and sunlight.

Costers Dancing was sketched on Epsom Downs, but it was painted in Sydney in 1940. Details are willingly sacrificed for the sake of breadth and monumentality, for, despite the liveliness of the action, these figures are meant to fill their measure of space with the positive insistence of sculpture. Rows of pearly buttons insist on every contour, carrying the eye about the rounded forms until we know each rise and fall as though our hands had actually touched them. Two women are dancing to the music of the accordion. With more energy than grace they lift their yellow-stockinged feet and prance about the grass, and the movement sets their coral ostrich plumes aquiver, their pearly buttons gleaming and fluttering like animated mosaics. Another woman has been dancing, but she has tired herself out, and she sits awkwardly like an oddly articulated doll. She has refreshed herself from a bottle, and in a moment she will remember to eat the banana she has peeled. Something in this figure catches the artist's imagination, and later on he made a separate study of her in *Derby Day*.

Perhaps the clearest evidence of a change in style is provided by a comparison between the 1937 sketch for *Saddle-My-Nag* and the final version painted in 1941.

Ills. 42, 43

He had seen a group of Irish servant-girls and their boy-friends playing the game in Hyde Park. As a schoolboy he too had played the same game, in which the players divided themselves into two teams, one of which became the 'nag' and the other the 'riders'. The object of the game is for the riders to attempt to make the 'nag' collapse. The losing team then becomes the 'nag'. It is a variation of that other old village-green game 'stacks on the mill'.

The sketch is painted with that 'heavy-handed strength' he so admired in Rembrandt and Van Gogh. The colour is warm, dark, and restricted; the paint is thick with descriptive impastos *Ill. 30* like the head of *The Sleeping Greek*, the tonal range is strong and dramatic and the lines are firmly stated. By contrast the final painting is touched in with great lightness and delicacy, the colour is fresh and spring-like, the tonal range is narrower, and the lines soften and blur in the atmosphere.

Something has been lost, something has been gained. Perhaps the raucous gusto of the sketch is truer to the earthy uninhibited spirit of the scene it describes. Though the observation is no less keen in the second version, it has lost something of the high-spirited liveliness of the original study. In the sketch the figures filled the picture area. Their bursting energy crowded the edges as though threatening to break the restraints that held them in. The game is tamer in the more considered version. It has almost become a landscape with figures at play. They have more space to play in, and consequently the game seems less urgent. It has lost its animal spirits and gained a vernal charm touched with nostalgia, for it records the memory of a lively moment rather than the liveliness of the moment itself. The girls in their diaphanous dresses are transformed by memory into hoydenish relatives of Botticelli's graceful Flora and queenly Primavera – a batch of lesser Olympians indulging in un-Olympian pastimes.

Before the war finishes Dobell will have painted a dozen *Ill. 63* great portraits, beginning in 1940 with *The Cypriot* based on *Ills. 76,* the London drawing and oil sketch, and culminating in that *75, 66* superb trio *Brian Penton, Joshua Smith*, and *The Billy Boy*. No comparable sequence of portraits has ever appeared in Australian art, nor would it be easy, or even possible to find their like anywhere else in the contemporary world, with the possible exception of some of Kokoschka's work and, in another medium, the portrait busts of Epstein.

78

46 Sunshower, Ile de la Cité, 1945

These are vintage years.

Landscapes are rare. He recalls his delight in London's parks with a charming study of *Aspen Trees* and in 1945 he came across a Paris sketch in his notebooks and painted the delightful *Sunshower, Ile de la Cité* from it. *Ill. 46*

Once he went to a Sunday crowded beach and saw a surf carnival. From his observations he painted a small picture in sun-bleached colours as formal and elegant as a ballet setting. Many years later he was to return to this subject and treat it with greater freedom and less stylized grace.

47 *The Tattooed Lady, 1941*

Carnival is a painting of extraordinary delicacy. Poses and groupings have the artificial feel of the studio about them. They are too elegant, too 'right' to be altogether convincing, but they are touched in with such breath-taking lightness and with such an exquisite sense of rhythm that one begins to think of the picture in terms of dancing, or of music. Two beautiful *tableaux* are linked by canvas screens that move across the picture like an *adagio* from a Beethoven quartet.

Dobell is attracted by the possibilities of this highly finished artificial elegance. We will see it again in the Rococo rhythms and stylish attenuations of his portrait of Jacqueline Crookston. It is at its best in the subtle, almost imperceptible, distortions of his *Elaine Haxton* portrait and at its least effective in the formal

Ill. 67

80

portraits of Lord and Lady Wakehurst. We can see it in its strangest form in *The Tattooed Lady* where a combination of grotesque distortion and formal elegance should have brought the picture to disaster – but doesn't. *Ill. 47*

Cool elegance leads him in one direction, warm earthiness in another. He was never an artist who could be happy following a single path. Interspersed among paintings as delicate and as

48 Pearl, 1940

stylized as Meissen china are others as uncompromisingly human as any he has ever painted.

Pearl is probably the most beautiful of all his nude paintings. It pictures a fat girl washing her feet – the sort of thing Degas delighted in painting; but Dobell's plump *Pearl* is so composed that she resembles a gleaming, pale pink, over-blown rose. An enclosed shape, limbs folded in like petals, soft textures and colour all combine to suggest a rose in full bloom. He has

49 Mother and Child, 1942

50 *Souvenir, 1943*

painted her with freely curving, sensuously rhythmical brush strokes, and the colours glow with a pearly lustre. One has only to compare it with the harsh, unforgiving realism of the 1936 *Toilette* to understand the range of Dobell's styles and the variety of his attitudes. He can adapt the very manner of his painting to the mood inspired by the subject.

Young Mother and *Mother and Child* are further examples of a more tender approach, but this tenderness never sinks into sentimentality. He sees the 'Young Mother' exactly as she is, a slatternly young woman feeding her child on the steps of an open doorway. The pose is ungainly and the expression on the face is certainly not the sort of thing that Raphael would have

Ill. 28

Ill. 49

wanted to paint, yet, despite the undercurrent of discontent and boredom, there is a touching intimacy in the scene.

Ill. 50   He is much harder on the young mother in *Souvenir*. One feels that the *Woman in a Hamburger* and the mother in *Souvenir* could have been the same woman, except that he has painted them in the wrong order – the 'After' preceding the 'Before'.

Dobell would not have had to move far from his flat in King's Cross to discover scenes and faces like the one he has recorded

Ill. 40   so vividly in *Woman in a Hamburger* – the finest of his Sydney genre paintings. Here again, the style is completely attuned to the subject. The paint fusses over the dressed-to-kill finery, but loosely and smudgily like the lady's morals. The knowing waiting, expression just perceptible behind the cosmetic mask is a masterpiece of observation. Like 'Mrs South Kensington' she is a type rather than an individual. From a hundred observations the artist has distilled the essence of a certain type of woman, but he has given the composite image all the characteristics of a unique personality. She is synthetic and real at the same time; she is completely believable because she is such a brilliant synthesis. She rests calmly with her left hand spread symbolically on her handbag. She may even be a little bored with waiting, bored perhaps by what she is waiting for, since she is obviously no novice. This is not the first time she has waited, nor will it be the last time. She is still, but the paint is fidgeting. While she pretends to concentrate on her cigarette she is sidespying and sizing.up the crowd around her. Perhaps she is looking into a mirror across the counter and sees herself reflected as she watches for the right one.

On second thoughts she can hardly be the same woman as the one in *Souvenir*. She would never be caught like that. And yet – ! Surely the father of the satyr-like child must have been just such a sailor as the one we half glimpse behind the waiting woman. Was ever a child painted with such a wickedly knowing face? So might the infant Nero have looked.

Ill. 51   In softer mood Dobell painted the *Prima Donna in Box* – a *tour de force* in which the singer's bulky form is shrouded in a

51 *Prima Donna in Box*, 1942

52 *Drawing for Russian Incident, 1942*

mist of paint without losing its weight or volume. She sits
listening to the music like a soft Gibraltar shrouded in misty
chiffon. He painted the charming little *Fair Haired Boy* with all
the innocence and freshness of youth, a complete contrast to
the little monster of *Souvenir*. Its delicacy reminds us of *Billy
Frost* though the pose, the rhythms, and the ordering of space
derives from *The Sleeping Greek*.

Only one of Dobell's paintings refers explicitly to the war.
His was not the kind of imagination that could be ignited by
someone else's experiences. He had to see and know for himself
before he could paint. Others, Delacroix for instance, could
read of Hamlet and poor Yorick's skull, and be moved to paint
a picture. Daumier could be incited to paint by a newspaper

86

53 Russian Incident, 1942

report of a brutal murder; but words, no matter how masterly their use, could rarely stir Dobell's creative imagination. He needs to start from visual facts. Once his eye has been caught by something – a shape, a colour, a texture, an expression, a movement, a gesture, a situation, an effect of light – his imagination is liberated. He can develop and invent in the most extraordinary way, provided the initial impetus comes from a visual experience.

Consequently, *Russian Incident* is unique among his paintings, for it was directly inspired by a newspaper report of an episode during the German army's invasion of Russia. Even so, it is possible that the real source of the painting lies in the artist's deep admiration for Goya. Needless to say, it is not actually based on

Ills. 52, 53

87

any particular work by the Spanish artist, but the theme, mood, general composition, and tonal arrangement has much in common with some of the 'Disasters of War' etchings. Indeed, it would be hard to paint a picture of this sort without being in debt to Goya.

By nature a gentle, sensitive person, Dobell detests violence. Only once does he portray it in his art and that, one suspects, is an act of homage to Goya's artistry. His real war paintings are of men engaged in constructive, or at least non-aggressive pursuits. Three of them are of cement workers, one shows a group of men loading ships at night, another the erection of a camouflage tree. We see workmen leaving an aerodrome at knocking-off time, and he takes us into a night recreation hut in a Civil Construction Corps Camp. Best of all he has given us two memorable portraits of men he has met on the job – the *Ills. 74, 66* shrewd, racy *Cement Worker* and the work-shy *Billy Boy*.

54 *Barrowmen, 1943*

55 *Barrowman, Perth, 1944*

56 *Emergency Loading at Night, Perth, 1944*

In all probability Dobell would never have painted genre pictures of this sort if left to follow his own inclinations. Significantly he never returned to them after the war was over.

His next pictures of men at work were of New Guinea natives gathering orchids, or thatching huts, and these were treated in an entirely different way. This does not mean that he was not interested in his subjects, or that he failed to make the most of them. His eye for significant movement and telling gesture allows him to extract the essence of each situation, and his technical mastery permits him to tackle the most difficult effects of light and composition with complete assurance.

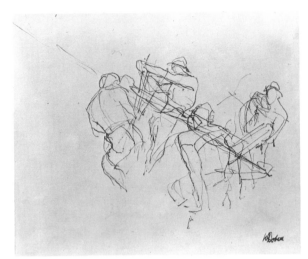

57
Four Men Working,
1943

58 Erecting Camouflage Tree, Menangle, 1944

59
The Concrete Workers,
1944

He is always interested in human activity, but the kind that interests him most is the kind that points up a state of mind, or reflects a quirk of personality. The men he painted in the C.C.C. genre group are too intent on their jobs to be anything but men at work. We know nothing about the *Barrowman, Perth* beyond his wiry capacity for work. What he feels or thinks is not disclosed, but his body arches up through the painting like a drawn bow, taut with straining energy. *Emergency Loading at Night, Perth* tells us even less about the men involved in the operation. The real theme of the painting is the flood of artificial light casting a strange luminosity over the wharf, barge, and workmen. Mysterious shadows filch substance from the figures. An electric glare catches a muscular back, haloes a head, or runs in forked lightning along an arm or a leg. A bollard throws a dark ray towards the foremost figures, blotting their feet in deep shadows.

Ill. 61

Ill. 55

Ill. 56

Many years later in the highlands of New Guinea he will again see night-time scenes that stir his imagination, but the magical firefly incandescence of *Kanana* is prefigured in the starker floodlighting of this picture. *Ill. 103*

Erecting Camouflage Tree, Menangle is the most elaborately constructed and highly finished of the series. Once again he achieves an effect of violent effort by the most classical means and once again, in the aerial figures in the nets, we are given the first hint of a theme that will find its fullest and most beautiful expression in the New Guinea *Thatchers*. *Ill. 104*

Characteristic of Dobell's use of form is the contrast between the four 'pullers' in the foreground and the two 'pushers' in the background. The sideways strain on the pullers seems to have stretched their bodies into abnormal breadth; the upward thrust of the pushers has narrowed their bodies into abnormal elongations.

60 *Concrete Consolidation Worker, Sydney Graving Dock, 1944*

Ordinarily Dobell uses distortion to heighten the emotional effect of a situation, or to draw attention to a physical or temperamental characteristic in a person; here he uses it as a means of stressing the nature of a physical action – the difference between pulling sideways and pushing upwards.

Ill. 60   *Concrete Consolidation Worker, Sydney Graving Dock* might
Ill. 55   well have been conceived as a complement to *Barrowman, Perth*. Both pictures are dominated by single figures. The barrowman's action results in a pose of great strength and beauty, but the concrete consolidator's job forces his body into a crouching spider-like attitude in which the natural rhythms are replaced by awkward and unexpected relationships of form.

Each of the six genre paintings tackles a different problem. The two remaining pictures are both concerned with crowd

61 *Night Recreation C.C.C. Camp, 1944*

62 Knocking-off Time, Bankstown Aerodrome, 1944

scenes, but the character of each is entirely different. *Knocking-off
Time, Bankstown Aerodrome* is a scene of intense activity. On   *Ill. 62*
the right a lorry load of workers streak homeward in the
gathering darkness – bicyclists and pedestrians crowd the
muddy road. In the foreground is a type who could have
modelled for Patrick White's hooligan, 'Bluey', in *Riders in the
Chariot*. The mood is one of haste and confusion, of snapping bad
temper or shouted ribaldries. Fittingly, the paint streaks and
splashes, the brush strokes jostle and badger each other, the
colour is worn out and grey.

   Night Recreation C.C.C. Camp is equally crowded but the   *Ill. 61*
mood is more relaxed, the jostling has fewer hard edges to it.
Light filters through the smoky air with a warm glow.

95

Ills. 74, 66 The Civil Construction Corps paintings culminate in *Cement Worker, Sydney Graving Dock* and *The Billy Boy* but these are portraits and should be considered among the other portraits of the period.

At this period of his life Dobell had not yet begun to attract many patrons. Few of the portraits were commissioned; most were painted because the artist was attracted by an appearance, or a temperament that presented a challenge to his expressive powers. It would be a mistake to think of these portraits as an orderly sequence through which the artist reached to an ever-increasing maturity.

Ill. 63
Ill. 75 The artist who painted *The Cypriot* at the beginning of the period is as fully mature as the one who painted *Joshua Smith* nearly four years later.

What emerges from the series is not a line of development but a map of the area of which he is master.

The Cypriot and *The Billy Boy* are stylistically dissimilar. It is easy enough to interpret the latter as a development from the former, but to do so would be to miss the whole point of Dobell's extraordinary talent.

By the time he arrived back in Australia he was like a virtuoso pianist who had mastered every kind of 'touch' and could use his mastery to interpret the spirit of the music. In his case the spirit of the music was the personality of his sitter.

Ills. 67, 66 An artist concerned only with external realities would have painted *Elaine Haxton* and *The Billy Boy* in a similar manner. He would have recorded his visual observations in a serviceable style and let it go at that. The quality of paint, the 'touch' of the brush, would hardly vary. But Dobell is not wholly, or even primarily, concerned about the way people look. He is far more interested in what they are – in the inner realities express-ing themselves through the sign language of gesture and behaviour, through the sound of their voices, the meaning of their words, and the unspoken meaning of their eyes!

There are times when he coaxes the forms and the personality out of the paint with a brush as caressing as a lover's touch.

63 *The Cypriot, 1940*

The paint glides over and around the object with an infinity of sliding touches, and each touch adds to our knowledge of the form and the spirit that inhabits it. He paints like a blind man knowing with his finger-tips. Each contact reveals a new facet of form, another subtlety of construction, another variation in texture, a deepening sense of character.

At other times his paint is more aggressive. The strokes embody the forms with bold assurance and the very look of the paint provides a key to the character of the sitter. This aspect of his art is most fully realized in the series of Helena Rubinstein portraits begun in 1957, but a comparison between *The Strapper* and *The Billy Boy* shows the subtlety of the interplay between appearance, personality, and paint.

Ill. 69 *The Strapper* was painted from a professional model who posed at the art school when Dobell taught there in 1941.

A strapper is a stable-hand. His job is to groom the horse, feed and water it, polish and tend the harness and, in general, see that his charge reaches the starting-line as glossy and pampered as a beauty queen.

Dobell has given his model an equine elegance; the forms are stretched and elongated to suggest the grace and speed of the racehorse. A mane of light chestnut hair stands out against the darker chestnut of the background, the paint is smooth, immaculate, taut, unfussy, and fastidious. There is no un-tidiness; the paint is brushed and groomed as meticulously as the horse's shining flanks.

Ill. 66 *The Billy Boy* is just the opposite. Dobell painted him in 1943.

Writer, Frank Clune, records the artist's reminiscences of the model in his book *Across the Snowy Mountains* (Angus & Robertson 1961). 'He was a Glasgow Irishman', he said, 'his name was Joe Westcott. He was more interested in political argument than boiling the billy – which was his only job. Whenever we were waiting for our tea at morning or afternoon smoko, Joe, a dinkum bush lawyer, was trying to shout someone else down in an ear-bashing contest, and we often had to boil our own billy. I painted him at Rathmines Air Base, where I

64 *Portrait of a Boy, 1943*

65 *Study for*
The Student, 1940

was working on camouflage with Joshua Smith and a lot of
other artists.'

From the Registrar-General's office Clune discovered the
following facts: 'Joseph Westcott, labourer, aged 69, died at
Stoney Creek, Toronto, about 28th January, 1956. Father was
a stonemason, deceased was born in Motherwell, Scotland,
was unmarried and lived about forty years in New South Wales.'

He sums it up by saying: 'In this magnificent oil painting of
the "downtrodden" working man, a gorilla with hairy torso,
Dobell has satirically epitomized the pannikin boss, a beer
swizzler – all brawn and no brain – who loafs on his mates. They
do all the hard yakka while Billy Boy looks on and on and on.'

6 *The Billy Boy*, 1943

Insight shows the artist what he is to paint, and intuition guides him to the way in which it would be best to paint it Knowing his subject, Dobell has allowed his paint to become as sloppy and amorphous as his sitter's personality. It slips about with oleaginous ease. Forms are as big and vague as the Billy Boy's arguments. Everything is loose, unmuscular, flabby, and puffed up with beer fat.

In every great painting, form and content are closely woven together. Even so, it would be hard to recall a painting in which the manner of the painting was so at one with the subject. This in itself, would be an achievement sufficient to single it out as one of the great portraits of our time, but our astonishment increases when we view it in the context of Dobell's other paintings – when we realize his extraordinary capacity to adapt his style to the service of so many different temperaments.

Picasso is a master of stylistic flexibility. So is Dobell. The difference between them stems from the fact that Picasso develops his repertory of styles for their own sake, pushing each one as far as it will go, then turning to another, while Dobell always uses his flexibility as a servant to visual or psychological realities. He has mastered so many nuances of approach because such mastery could make him a better servant to the truth. And truth, for Dobell, always hinges on something seen and on the host of deductions and divinations that surround a visual experience with an invisible aura of significance.

Ill. 63   *The Cypriot* was the first portrait the artist painted after his return. If we compare it with his earlier painting of the same
Ill. 30   model – *The Sleeping Greek* – we will be struck by the greater formality of the later work. The pose has an almost hieratic stiffness, the sort of pose he was to use with astonishing effect
Ill. 115   in his 1957 portrait of Dame Mary Gilmore. Having once caught him asleep and off guard, Dobell now presented him staring straight out of the canvas directly into our eyes. His eyes are watchful and his hands, drooping from the arm-rests, are full of controlled nervous energy. The stillness of the pose is deceptive; it cannot disguise his alertness.

67 Elaine Haxton, 1941

Dobell loves to achieve his effects through a paradox. We have seen how he went about the problem of showing the inner character of the sleeping Greek in the dynamic line of the pose. Here he reverses the process. Through a relatively static pose he has shown us what energy it costs an energetic man to be inactive.

Almost geometric in its precision, everything leads our attention to the face and the hands. It is a face that would have interested El Greco – dark, intense eyes, narrow bones, a long nose branching into heavy arching eyebrows, a sensuous mouth, yet an overall expression of detachment. El Greco would have tilted the head towards heaven and rolled the eyes upward in ecstasy, but such a face would have seemed quite natural in one of his martyrdoms.

The sitter's left hand was taken from a detailed study for which Joshua Smith posed.

68
Capt G.U. 'Scotty' Allan, 1941

69 The Strapper, 1941

During the next two years Dobell painted five more out-standing portraits, four of which are closely related in style. *Ills. 63, 69* Both *The Cypriot* and *The Strapper* are alive with vivid colour. Now his palette becomes more restrained. *Elaine Haxton,* *Ills. 68,* *Captain G. U. 'Scotty' Allan, James Cook,* and *Norman Schureck* *70, 71* are all painted in cool blue-green harmonies. The touch is soft and coaxing, and the outlines tend to blur in a hazy atmosphere.

Ill. 67   *Elaine Haxton* is one of the most decorative, and certainly the most theatrical, of all his portraits, and this is fitting since Elaine Haxton is a fine decorative artist in her own right and has done some of her most telling work for the theatre, especially for the ballet.

Only very occasionally does Dobell go to any trouble to present his sitter against a definite background. Usually he is content to concentrate on the face and figure and to put in only such things as are necessary to explain the pose. Most often the background is an indefinite space coloured to enhance the drama of the pose or the character of the sitter.

Most of the portraits with descriptive backgrounds are of women. *Jacqueline Crookston* (1940), *Elaine Haxton* (1941), *Lady* *Ills. 90, 119* *Wakehurst* (1944), *Margaret Olley* (1948), and *Woman in a Salon* (Helena Rubinstein – 1960) are examples of this elaboration. *Ill. 75* Among the male portraits only *Joshua Smith* (1943) has been placed so specifically in a particular environment. *Elaine Haxton* and *Lady Wakehurst* are presented in landscape settings, but they are imaginary landscapes designed to enhance and com-plement the central figure. The landscape is used as a studio prop, as it was in certain portraits by Reynolds and Gainsborough.

Miss Haxton's pose is highly artificial and the artist makes no attempt to persuade us that it is a logical position for the body to assume. He does not explain what the right arm is resting on, or account for the curious twist of the shoulders. We can only assume that she is sitting on a low bank, though her shoes do not seem to rest on the ground – rather does she look as though she was floating weightlessly against a sylvan

106

71 *Norman Schureck, 1942*

background. Even the clothes she wears are curiously out of place in such a setting, unless she is drifting by on her way to an elaborate theatrical garden-party.

The whole painting has a dream-like quality, a sense of charming unreality such as ballet might create. We can imagine her listening to distant music, and the music she hears would have to be Tchaikovsky. This would account for her training forward to catch the sound, for the rapt, smiling, listening expression on her face, and for the implications of buoyant movement in the pose.

Stylistically it is similar to the final version of *Saddle-My-Nag* which was painted about this time. It marks the furthest limits of an aspect of Dobell's nature that is the reverse of his robust realism. It is his most successful attempt to express his enjoyment of stylized elegance. *Ill. 43*

'*Scotty' Allan*, *James Cook*, and *Norman Schureck* are almost conventional portraits by comparison. All three tell us a great deal about the sitter. Each looks out at us with a quizzical, appraising, and revealing stare. If we were to meet them for the first time we would meet them as people we already knew quite well. *Ills. 68, 70, 71*

The Student is an exception during this period. For one thing it evokes a Venetian splendour of colour with its warmly glowing reds. The attenuation of its forms takes us back to *The Strapper*, but it is much freer in treatment. *Ill. 65*

Ill. 69

As if to counterbalance the luxury of the colour, Dobell has selected a pose of rigid frontality. The sitter is drawn in with an almost archaic lack of movement. But for the triumphantly singing colour and the expression of the face we would be reminded of a primitive cult figure, so symmetrically disposed are the forms.

It is the expression that rivets our attention. Under a mass of curly black hair as formal as a ritual wig, the forehead furrows in uncertainty, the eyes ask questions, the mouth purses on the point of speech, the shoulders sag in acceptance. With a body as still as a watched animal the face alone is alive, though it is animated only by perplexities.

How different this is to the physical arrogance of the *Cement Worker, Sydney Graving Dock* with his big, cement-grey workman's hands dragging at his elastic braces in a characteristic gesture. Shrewd sun-wrinkled eyes survey the world without doubts about its meaning, or about his rightful place in the scheme of things. *Ill. 74*

109

Could any portrait be further removed from the mood and spirit of *Elaine Haxton*? Yet they are separated by only three years. The distance between them indicates the extent of the domain Dobell has made his own.

With the remaining two portraits of this period, the artist returned to the brilliant colour schemes of *The Cypriot* and *The Strapper*.

72 *Study for David Lloyd Jones, 1943*

Both *Brian Penton* and *Joshua Smith* were painted within a Ills. 76, 75 few months of one another in 1943, and both were entered for the Archibald Prize for Portraiture at the beginning of 1944, the latter being awarded the prize.

Today portraiture is sick with an illness that has brought it to so low an ebb that many have despaired of its survival as a valid category of art. The declining vigour of this proud category has worried those who worry about such things for fifty years or more

There is no mystery about the disease.

A portrait painter has two masters – his model and his artistic conscience, which is based on those aesthetic values he accepts as true. He aims to create a work of art that is also the likeness of an individual in a physical and psychological sense.

Sometimes in the history of art it is relatively easy for the artist to fulfil both aims successfully, but there are times, and ours is one of them, when this duality of aims creates almost insuperable difficulties.

Great portraiture occurs in those periods when art is most concerned with the visible world (there was no problem in Imperial Rome or in Europe between the fifteenth and nineteenth centuries) and is weakest when its chief concern is with spiritual conditions, inner values, abstract concepts, the exploration of feelings, motives, and states of mind.

Today these latter conditions prevail and for almost a hundred years the artist has been investigating territory that has taken him further and further away from the realities of visual experience.

So, portraiture is stricken because the artist is too far out to be able to make an easy compromise. The gap is too wide. The compromise is uneasy and tentative.

In the forty-two years of its existence the Archibald Prize for Portraiture has only once been won by a painting that seemed to point the way to a remedy. Dobell's *Joshua Smith* was Ill. 75 a great painting and a great portrait.

73 *Sketch for Cement Worker, 1943*

74 *Cement Worker, Sydney Graving Dock, 1944*

Ill. 76 It, and the *Brian Penton*, marked the furthest limit of thi
extraordinarily gifted artist's attempt to bring the portrait back
into the realm of living art. Line, design, form, and colou
were pushed further towards Expressionism than he had eve
attempted before, and he was not to repeat the experimen
until he painted Dame Mary Gilmore and Helena Rubinstein
many years later.

Dobell did not paint at all for a year after the calamitou
court case that followed the *Joshua Smith* award, and when he
started again it was to landscape that he turned at first.

What might have happened if Dobell had not been diverted
from the line he was then pursuing is a question that must
trouble all who are concerned for the future of portraiture.

CHAPTER FOUR

The Court Case: 1944

Late in December 1943 Dobell entered the portrait of Joshua *Ill. 75* Smith for the Archibald Prize. Early in January 1944 the Trustees of the National Art Gallery of New South Wales awarded it the prize and in doing so sparked off a controversy that culminated in a court case without precedent in Australian history. Not only was it to have a profound effect on Dobell as a person and as an artist, but it was to become a testing-ground where the forces of conservatism were marshalled in full strength against the budding energies of the modern movement.

Issue was joined when two unsuccessful exhibitors, Mary Edwards and Joseph Wolenski took legal action to set aside the Trustees' decision. Both were well-known portraitists and members of the reactionary Royal Art Society.

Mary Edwards specialized in highly coloured, romanticized studies of South Sea Islanders, and in portraits with an extraordinarily high sugar content; Wolenski was a rigidly academic rule follower. Prompted to action by their conviction that the painting was not a true portrait as required under the terms of the Archibald Award, they moved the Supreme Court of New South Wales to set aside the Trustees' decision in the following claim:

'It is alleged that the picture is not a portrait but a caricature of Joshua Smith, bearing a certain degree of resemblance to him but having features distorted and exaggerated. Joshua Smith is a man of normal human aspect and proportion, and is not misshapen or deformed, but the picture is a representation of a person whose body, limbs, and features are grotesquely at variance with normal human aspect and proportions. It is apparent that the said picture does not represent any attempt on the part of the defendant Dobell to make a likeness of Smith, but on the contrary, represents the result of an endeavour to depict him in a distorted and caricatured form.'

The Plaintiffs engaged the services of Mr Barwick, K.C., now Sir Garfield Barwick, and Dr Louat, later a Trustee of the Art Gallery until his death. Mr Kitto, K.C., and Mr Kerrigan appeared for the Trustees and Mr Dwyer, K.C., and Mr Conybeare appeared for the Defendant William Dobell. The case was heard before Mr Justice Roper in the Supreme Court of New South Wales in Equity, between 23 and 26 October 1944.

Mr Barwick called on Mr Dwyer to produce the picture in question, which then became Exhibit D.

First witness for the Plaintiffs was Mr J. S. MacDonald who began by establishing his credentials as an authority. Although he was then retired he had a distinguished record as an art administrator and critic in New South Wales and Victoria. He stated that his training had covered twelve years, six in Melbourne and six in France. From 1928 to 1936 he had been Director of the National Art Gallery of New South Wales and from 1936 to 1941 Director of the National Gallery of Victoria.

He then went on to say: 'I am familiar with the development of portraiture. There is quite a distinct category of art which one can call portraiture; it is very well defined. It is differentiated from other forms in a particular way. It is a special thing, just as a sonnet would be in literature. You have to have certain definite limits within which you work. There has to be a balanced characterization of the subject and as to the featural details and proportions it should be objective, though not to the extent that it prevents a certain amount of subjectiveness on the part of the painter from entering into it. Within that gamut you have to work, and you cannot take liberties because your ego is tugging at you.'

Mr MacDonald said he was familiar with the history of portraiture and quoted some examples from Flanders, Greece, Egypt, China, and India to prove the point.

Q. You have told me you are familiar with the development of portraiture subsequent to Van Eyck, and oil painting?

116

A. Yes.

Q. You are familiar with the various portraits that are hung in the different galleries?

A. Yes.

Q. Do you find in any of them any element of distortion of the figure or features?

A. No, none.

Q. Does that go for the art of other people you have mentioned?

A. Yes, it is universal. The world has agreed on the definition of portraiture – it excludes that.

Q. Is a distinct line drawn between portraiture and caricature?

A. Yes, definitely.

Mr MacDonald then launched into a brief history of portraiture in Italy, Holland, and England.

In reply to Mr Dwyer's question: 'What is the date of the last good portraitist?' Mr MacDonald answered: 'Lawrence, I think he died in 1832.' (Sir Thomas Lawrence 1769–1830.) Mr Barwick: You have seen Mr Smith before today?

A. Yes.

Q. Can you see him from where you are now?

A. Yes, I can see him.

Q. Have you seen Exhibit D before?

A. Yes, I have seen it before.

Q. In your opinion is Exhibit D a portrait of Joshua Smith?

A. I do not know how far –

Q. You can say Yes or No?

A. No.

Q. Would you be able to tell us what it is in relation to him?

A. I think it is a pictorial defamation of character.

Q. If you were given the job of hanging it, if you had to classify it in some way, what would you classify it as?

A. I would call it a fantasy, a satirical caricature.

Q. The human face and form are put to various uses in painting?

A. Yes.

Q. Tell us some of the things they are used for.

A. In the composition of any picture the human form comes

n, whether nude, or draped, in costume, for historical purposes, and allegorical purposes, parables, conversational pieces. Its uses are very great, but portraiture is specific.

Q. The use of it in a portrait is distinct from its use in a specific way?

A. I think of a sonnet, that has to have an octave and a sextet. You have to keep within those limits. You are not free. Hals painted A Man Playing a Mandolin – that is the Mandolin Player. That is not a portrait. A man drinking a pewter pot of beer is a token; that is not a portrait. He knows what he has got to call it. If he wants to paint a portrait he says to that man 'Put that pot down beside you and I will paint you as you are, not as you are at an instantaneous moment.'

Q. You say it is not in your opinion a portrait of Joshua Smith; are you able to tell us your specific reason or reasons for saying so?

A. Yes. It is the spirit in which the thing is painted. If I had never seen Mr Smith before, and someone said to me 'Here is a picture of a portrait painter', I would say 'No, that man could not paint a portrait.' I know Joshua Smith can paint a portrait because I have handled his portraits. He sent in to the Archibald Prize when I was at the National Gallery. I know his work. That is a poor creature.

Q. Because of the physical proportions, that is one of your reasons for saying it is not a portrait?

A. Yes.

Q. Is there any other reason you give for thinking it is not a portrait?

A. A portrait allows of your consideration, your scrutiny. You do not feel as if it was your bounden duty to ring for the ambulance, as you do when you see that sort of thing.

Q. Is there any other reason you desire to give for thinking this is not a portrait of this man?

A. It looks like an elf-person, a person sick in body and brain. Not a man who could paint a portrait fit for entry into the Archibald Prize.

76 Brian Penton, 1943

Q. What in your view is the essential of a portrait?
A. First of all it has to be a balanced likeness of an actual person.
Q. In relation to Exhibit D are you able to say whether or not that is a likeness – leave out the word 'balanced' for a moment – of the sitter?
A. I do not think it is.
Q. In particular would you count it a balanced likeness?
A. No, very unbalanced, a caricature – *caricare*; to overload.

The cross-examination began with the question whether 'The category of portraiture is as clearly defined as a sonnet?' When pressed for a generally accepted definition MacDonald was unable to produce one and defended his vagueness by claiming that painters were not in the habit of 'reducing to formulae the meaning of their art'.

Still under pressure, he retreated from his previous dogmatic position to the extent of admitting that 'there need not be unanimity [of opinion] as to the resemblance between the picture and the sitter in order that the picture may qualify as a portrait'.
Q. If some of those who know the sitter see a likeness, and some do not, is the picture a portrait or not?
A. I should say it would be a portrait.
Q. What I put to you earlier would be correct. That whether a picture is a portrait or not must be a matter of the individual opinion of those who consider it?
A. It is hard to answer. Yes, I suppose so.

Later on the question of characterization arose.
Q. Looking at the picture you would conclude that it was painted from an actual sitter?
A. Yes.
Q. Knowing Mr Joshua Smith, may I suggest that it is not entirely devoid of some resemblance to him?
A. That is so.
Q. Would you go so far as to suggest there is no element in that picture of any attempt to portray character?
A. Yes. There is on one side – that is timidity.

Q. You get that information from the picture?

A. Yes.

Q. Would it be going too far to suggest that it indicates some other characteristic possibly? Would you think it suggests a man who has been through a considerable amount of ill-health?

A. It looks to me as if he had been cornered by the New York police and beaten with a piece of lead pipe for not coming clean.

Q. Leaving aside any attempt to be humorous, I am asking you, do you see any suggestion in that picture that the sitter was a man who had suffered from ill-health?

A. Yes, certainly.

Q. I put it to you that it suggests a man who, although having suffered from ill-health, has not been defeated in his spirit?

A. It never occurred to me.

Q. Have a good look at it now. Would it be consistent with your opinion of that picture that there is a man who has suffered greatly but has not been defeated and still has an unconquerable spirit?

A. No. On prompting it might. I do not know, but it did not occur to me.

Q. I want to see whether now when I suggest it you think that is a fair suggestion?

A. He looks fearful; he looks apprehensive – that seems to be overriding.

Q. Would you say but not cowed by his fears?

A. He looks as if he is used to it.

Q. And not cowed by it, I suggest?

A. His attitude, sitting up, looks as if he was facing the music, but apart from that, I do not see that he is playing the part of Invictus.

Q. Would you think there was any air of wistfulness about him?

A. Yes.

But MacDonald would not budge from his opinion that the work was a caricature even though he admitted that it was done by an accomplished artist.

On the second day of the hearing John Young took the stand for the Plaintiffs. In 1925 he started the Macquarie Gallery in Sydney with Basil Burdett as partner, and before his retirement in 1939 he had done much to encourage such early Post-Impressionists as Roland Wakelin and Roy de Maistre. He had only just resigned from the position of Acting Director of the National Gallery of New South Wales. Young thought the portrait painter worked under very great limitations.

Q. What are the limitations?

A. I feel that in a portrait it is a compact between the sitter and the artist. If I may put it this way, I think the sitter provides the goods, and the artist uses them, and between them they create a third thing, a work of art; and that work of art is shared equally, the responsibilities in that work of art are shared equally between the sitter and the painter.

Q. In what relation does the work of art stand in regard to the two of them?

A. It stands as the consummation of their contributions to its achievement.

Q. In the interpretation of the sitter, is he limited in any way by the physical objective presence of the sitter, or is he unlimited?

A. Obviously he is limited.

The following extract throws interesting light on the situation in Australian art just after the First World War.

Q. You know, do you not, that abroad a school or schools of art developed from 1908 to 1910 in which emphasis was placed on subjectivity, the artist being free to express himself without regard to representation?

A. Yes.

Q. So far as Australia is concerned, do you recall when that school first became operative in any sense, in Australia?

A. I do. I remember its exact origin.

Q. Can you tell us the year?

A. About 1919. Reproductions in which there was the acknowledgement of modern ideas came upon Sydney mainly through the magazine *Colour*. Up to that point I do not think there was really a modern picture anywhere, at any rate in Sydney.

Q. As far as concerns the practice of painting in accordance with those ideas, when did that begin in Australia?

A. The actual practice – I bought the first two modern pictures that were shown in Australia. They were shown by a man named Gren who went to America. There were three things, one by de Maistre, one by Wakelin, and one by Gren. He was making experimentations in the modern manner.

Q. What year would that be?

A. That would be 1916. That was merely a students' show which had not become recognized. They were considered quite gone mad.

Young was not wholly in favour of the suit. He doubted very much whether a matter of art could be settled in a law suit. He believed that it was practically impossible to so define or to limit a disputed matter of art as to get some satisfactory answer that would settle the matter once and for all.

Later, in commenting on the portrait, Young describes it as a biological absurdity. 'I think that no being could live like that. I think I have seen something like that. I remember seeing in a textbook of psychiatry, some pictures of some poor sub-human creatures – who had been allowed to live and maintain one posture – and they developed very strange proportions. But they were sub-human.'

Q. And this reminds you of some of those illustrations?

A. Slightly, I am afraid.

The evidence of the two art experts was followed by that of a medical practitioner; Dr Vivian Benjafield, whose opinions were very explicit, said that the painting represented 'the body of a man who had died in that position and had remained in that position for a period of some months and had dried up'. He also said: 'The normal human neck has seven cervical vertebrae in it, and I think there would have to be at least ten to get that length of neck.'

In the cross-examination Dr Benjafield admitted that he

knew nothing about art and that the colour, eyes and mouth, were different to those of a dead man.

The case for the Defendants opened with the swearing in of Frank Medworth, who was the lecturer-in-charge of the Department of Art in the Sydney Technical College and Acting Director of the National Art Gallery of New South Wales.

He claimed that the portrait painter had the right to use his imagination in representing the characteristics of his sitter. 'If Van Dyck painted the picture of a kingly personage it would be a kingly personage at all costs, however insignificant that person looked in the flesh. He had to paint a Royal Personage. He was a Royal painter.'

He admitted that the portrait is markedly exaggerated – perhaps more exaggerated than is customary in the painting of portraits. 'It is', he said, 'a matter of the preference of the artist who chose this particular symbol for depicting the individual. This is not a commercial portrait. This is a portrait or picture painted by the artist of a person to satisfy himself.'

He goes on to say that distortion 'has always been employed by artists from the commencement of time to describe the character of the thing depicted. One has to select; one does not put everything in, one puts in the essentials. One makes a lot of some essentials, perhaps, and one subordinates the others. That is the artist's job. It is a metaphor rather than a facsimile, within the limits of his medium.'

Mr R. Haughton James stressed the importance of colour in the painting. The colour gave him an impression of slight unease.

During the cross-examination Mr Barwick asked: 'What do the flattened-off ears tell you?'

A. I am sorry – I am not a doctor or a carpenter.

Q. What did you get out of that picture – what did the ears tell you?

A. They are part of the whole.

Q. How do they help the whole?

A. What would one word tell you out of the Lord's Prayer?

Q. Do the ears tell you something in connection with the whole?

A. Yes – as one brick is part of the whole building. This is a picture, a work of art, a portrait of Smith.

Q. What does the mark under the left eye tell you about his character?

A. Nothing, I think.

Q. Does that help in the whole at all?

A. You give a small item such as the number of slats in this chair – I get no particular significance from the eye. The total conveys the impression.

Q. And in order to get this message from the picture you need to take in the entire canvas?

A. Certainly, because it is not only a portrait but a work of art.

Q. Background and everything?

A. Certainly.

In the opinion of sculptor, Lyndon Dadswell, a portrait should be 'a personal interpretation of your particular reaction to the subject – and it must be a work of art'. He maintained that different people would have different reactions to an individual according to their experience and knowledge of him. 'If a mask reproduction were taken of a subject it is quite on the cards that very few people would recognize that mask as that particular person.' He did not believe that there were rules in art. 'If I am going to allow that I have a personal point of view, then I must allow Mr Dobell that same licence. You go to Mr Dobell because you like the way Mr Dobell produces a picture that is a portrait – you go to Mr Joshua Smith because you like the way he does it, and so on.'

The next witness for the Defendants was Paul Haefliger, the art critic for the *Sydney Morning Herald*. He thought it was essential that a portraitist should picturize the man whom he is painting. 'Nevertheless, I do not think it of supreme importance that an absolute likeness is to be achieved. Through his reactions he [the artist] may ultimately give a clearer picture of himself. That is a trait which is common in all portraiture.

*77 Study for
Joshua Smith, 1943*

When you look through the old masters you will find that every
artist has his so-called type. There is the Leonardo type, there
is in modern times the Picasso type. Any great painter has a type.
Within his type he creates a portrait. I think ultimately you
will find that these portraits as such are to a certain extent
fallacious. They are reflections of the artist rather than a portrayal because the artist can only know himself thoroughly.
Take the physical features of the sitter. From that the artist can
possibly deduce the essential character of the inner being of the
sitter. I would say that the essential nature of art is something
that the artist himself is not fully aware of. The thing that
makes art is the spirit of the picture and the spirit is nothing
tangible. It cannot be put into words. What is the spirit of man?
You say a man is alive and you conclude that he has a moving

spirit within himself; but you cannot lay your hands on the essential spirit. I think that that point has been overlooked in this inquiry because artists have been asked to give definitions of something which is undefinable. I feel that a portrait is painted within the idiom of the painter's idea; that is to say, roughly, his school. It is a vague term, but in art most terms are very vague, including portraiture. Painters more or less are put into a class. Sometimes they transgress it but it is within that range that they paint.'

He went on to say that a Cubist painting by Picasso would not be a physical likeness of a photographic nature but would be concerned within the Cubist idiom and created out of the artist's knowledge of Cubism.

'Dobell', he said, 'is really what might be termed an Expressionist. He stresses the forms to express an emotion. You would term El Greco an Expressionist. He uses an emotion to express an idea, and he exaggerates that emotion. Rembrandt is an Expressionist, and he will transgress from the purely physical to express an emotion, and he will exaggerate. You will also find it in Goya and in Cézanne, to a certain extent, and in Picasso and Soutine and Rouault. Mr Dobell works within his limitations, therefore certain avenues are open to him. If he was a severe Classicist he could not exaggerate the way he exaggerates here. He would come within more mathematical formulae, a more architectural formula. It would not be the formula of the Impressionist and he could not elongate to that extent. The portrait now shown [Cézanne's *The Red Vest*] is one of the great masterpieces of the last century, and is much more exaggerated than Dobell's arm, and yet this portrait is acknowledged by Europe as one of the great masterpieces of Cézanne. You can see for yourself that this elongated arm and the break in the arm is something that Mr Dobell never allowed himself to do. He probably did not wish to do it. He might pause and say he did not dare to do it. This is a much greater example of exaggeration. It was painted many years ago – I do not know the exact date but it is at least fifty years ago.'

Q. What is that painting known as?
A. It is called *The Red Vest*. You may say that a thing that is called *The Red Vest* is not a portrait, but on the other hand, Cézanne never called it *The Red Vest*. That was a title which was given afterwards. Cézanne was concerned with a young person of the district in which he lived, and he painted his portrait. The title you give to the portrait is immaterial. If Cézanne had called it *The Red Vest* it would still be immaterial. This work is a portrait because it particularizes a certain sitter.

'In the Dobell picture the ears were referred to by one witness. There is a certain exaggeration of Joshua Smith's ears, but they are in themselves not more exaggerated than any other part. They are consistent with the whole exaggeration of the whole picture. I think every feature has slight exaggeration to an astoundingly similar degree. That gives a uniformity of expression to the whole portrait. I think the likeness in this portrait is considerable, but even if it had not been it could still have been a portrait; and we are not able to prove that the other portraits were absolute likenesses of those people. In the case of Rembrandt, who is one of the greatest portraitists of all time, his contemporaries complained that his portraits were not like them, that he did not get a likeness.'

Concluding, Haefliger pointed out that portraiture was a branch of art in which the revolutionary changes occurring in art over the past thirty or forty years would also occur.

Douglas Dundas, head teacher of life painting and drawing at the Sydney Technical College was the next to give evidence.

'Broadly speaking', he said, 'there are two different methods of approach to portrait painting. One, and this one has had a considerable vogue in Australia, is that in which the artist poses his sitter, sets up his canvas, and proceeds to make a visual record of the shapes of light and shade and of colour which the sitter presents to his eye. This particular tradition in portraiture is to a large extent derived from that great portrait painter Velazquez – perhaps indirectly; in Australia it has been to some extent derived from the portraits of Raeburn, who worked

very much by what I would call the light and shade method
There is a very good example – perhaps there are more than
one – of his work in the Melbourne Gallery, and artists of the
Melbourne school have been very much influenced in their
portrait work by these paintings of Raeburn. The second
method of approach is more through drawing and the sense of
construction. The artist may work from drawings or he may
work directly from the sitter, but the first line of departure in
his work is through drawing, and when I speak of drawing,
speak of drawing in the constructive sense and not in the
imitative sense.'

After noting the importance of the constructional approach
in Dobell's portrait he continued: 'Early Italian artists and early
Flemish artists did not work nearly so much by light and shade
as the artists of the seventeenth century. The development
towards visual facts, as revealed by light and shade, was a
steady one from the time of Giotto onwards. Roughly the first
one hundred or one hundred and fifty years of Italian painting
after the beginning of the Renaissance was marked by painting
which relied less upon the extent of light and shade than upon
the artist's conception of the form of his subject. Anyway, there
is a purer understanding of form in those works than there is in
the later works where artists became enamoured of the effect
of light and shade, of the drama of light and shade as it fell upon
their subject-matter.'

'Velazquez is the great master in the light and shade method
He is not, however, devoid of an understanding of form in its
purer sense as understood by the earlier Italians. Perhaps the
greatest master of all in the interpretation of humanity as
revealed under conditions of light and shade is Rembrandt, and
yet I would not say for one moment that all painting by Rem
brandt is concerned with light and shade only, because the
painter is really wielding, as it were, the baton in an orchestra
His job is to co-ordinate the various elements, both material
and intellectual, which he uses.

'The portrait painter has to bring about a co-ordination

etween so many different elements. He has the sitter. He has first of all a blank canvas, and from these two elements, by his own skill, he has eventually to produce a work of art which will be known as a portrait. I would say that he has to consider the likeness of his sitter. By likeness I don't mean only a likeness to the features of the head of the sitter, but to his general physical bearing as well. If he feels that he wishes to stress certain characteristics, he will do so, but first of all he has to have all the problems of creating on this blank canvas an image – an image which will be satisfactory as a portrait and as a work of art, and to create that image he has to consider the physical fact of the sitter, and the material facts of canvas, paint, and brushes, and the intellectual facts or factors of the design, by drawing or characterization, by tonal values of recession and of envelopment of the sitter, his position in space with air surrounding him. He has to consider the illumination of the picture, and he has to consider the colour. Now all these various elements are very difficult to combine satisfactorily in a work of art. A great many portraits, I think, are painted without taking a great deal of account of some, at any rate, of these elements. They may achieve a certain likeness or resemblance to the sitter, but they will be lacking in that profundity which comes to a work of art which is produced by a man who is capable of co-ordinating all these different elements in his picture. Just getting a likeness alone would not altogether constitute portraiture in my opinion.'

Finally Dobell, himself, went into the box and his evidence is worth quoting in detail.

To Mr Dwyer: 'I am one of the Defendants in this suit. I painted the portrait which is an exhibit in court. [Indicating Exhibit D.] I began my study of painting in the year 1924 at the Julian Ashton Art School. I was twenty-four then.'

Q. Was it prior or subsequent to that point of time in your life that you were associated with the firm of architects?

A. I began architecture at the age of sixteen and I was still an architect when I finished my studies in Sydney in 1929. I

remained for four years at the Julian Ashton School. In 192
I won the Travelling Scholarship awarded by the New Sout
Wales Society of Artists. That entitled me to further my studie
in England. I studied in London in the Slade School at th
London University under Professor Henry Tonks and Wilso
Steer, O.M.

Q. Professor Henry Tonks – what was his position at that time

A. He was regarded as one of the best teachers of draughtsman
ship in England.

Q. Wilson Steer – what was his position?

A. Wilson Steer was a teacher of painting and had about th
highest reputation as a painter at that time. He was a landscap
painter and a painter of portraits.

Q. Whilst you were at the Slade School, did you receive privat
tuition from Sir William Orpen?

A. Yes; I used to visit Sir William and he guided me in m
drawing, but advised me not to paint under him because h
did not want to influence my style too much.

Q. Whilst you were there did you win certain prizes i
connection with the school?

A. Yes, I shared second prize for draughtsmanship with
German youth and I received first prize in painting of the figure

Q. Did you exhibit at the Royal Academy?

A. Yes, I was 'hung' – in 1933 I think it was.

Q. I think you remained in England for a period of ten year
returning to this country in 1939?

A. During that period I was following my art in England, an
at various periods on the Continent; I was studying in England
When I gave up personal tuition at the Slade I continued to worl
on my own. I had to make a living and I illustrated a magazine
The Passing Show. Then I returned to Sydney and I took up
position of teaching draughtsmanship at the Sydney Technica
College; I was a part-time teacher. I accepted that position fo
about two years. Subsequent to that I was in the Civil Con
struction Corps as a camouflage labourer. Whilst I was ther
I was associated with Mr Joshua Smith. I knew him prior t

132

that; I knew Joshua when I first came back from London.

Q. This entry for the Archibald Prize – was that a serious work of portrait painting as far as you were concerned?

A. Well, I would not have exhibited it otherwise.

Q. And for the purposes of your work – and particularly for the purposes of painting a portrait of Mr Smith, what was the approach – what did you seek to obtain, and how far, in your opinion, did you succeed in obtaining that?

A. I knew Joshua – for four or five years, just meeting him casually. I did not really know him. I respected him and I still respect him, but I always regarded him as a rather diffident type of person and one who naturally seems to call for people's sympathy; but when I worked with him as a camouflage labourer, I had to share the same camp with him for almost twelve months, and I got to know his real character. I found that there was a determination that amounted to stubbornness.

Q. Did you endeavour to make manifest his character as you understood it, in this portrait?

A. Yes, that was my aim – as well as the visual.

Q. As far as Mr Smith's dignity or determination was concerned, was that what you sought to bring out in the work?

A. Not only that – I think I succeeded in sticking to my gun as a draughtsman and constructing a picture worthy of the name of a work of art, and I don't think I have distorted to the extent that other witnesses have suggested.

Q. Why did you resolve on that arrangement of the figure? Is there any significance in that?

A. Joshua has a habit, when he is very determined, and determined to gain his point, of sitting very erect and saying 'I will go to Curtin [the Prime Minister] if necessary' to get his point. He is a very determined person and I admire him for it and I tried to show that.

Q. Did you regard that as an attitude which would bring out what you regarded as one of his characteristics?

A. Joshua naturally sits in a chair that way; I like to know my sitters for at least a month before I begin to make studies for

134

paintings of them, and I had noticed Joshua's characteristic attitudes. He often visited me and sat in that particular chair.

Q. What significance did you intend in regard to the hands?

A. Joshua naturally sits and clasps his hands, and I tried to make the most of that feature of him, and it helped in the design, which is very important in a big painting. It helped me to build up the pyramidal, sculptural shape of the thing in the light. A lot of people have said that colour is not necessary, but students spend several years at least learning colour so I fail to see why they should dispense with it. If it is not necessary why aren't the Archibald prizes painted in black and white?

Q. The pyramidal effect of which you speak – was that achieved partly by the posture of the arms and limbs?

A. I have made use of Joshua's very long arms and have possibly exaggerated them. I admit a slight exaggeration and I have made use of them as a base for my pyramidal design.

Q. What do you say as to the construction, apart from the question of light and shade?

A. Mr Dundas spoke of two methods of portrait painting – one was the light and shade method, the other was the construction method. Mr Barwick seemed to give the impression that the second method was the ethereal one which needed no basic construction. You will find that this is the only one that has a basic construction, because you have to know the figure and you have to draw the figure, no matter what the position of the light. At the Slade School we began drawing in the morning a figure of a person with the light on one side of it, and to prevent us getting cheap imitation by light, it was switched to the other side of the room later on. It prevented us getting cheap light and shade effects as a camera does. You had to know the figure thoroughly. I have an example of a study here [indicating], my first study for Joshua Smith's portrait, and you will see I have not deviated from my first constructional form, the constructional form for his head.

Q. Having made your decision as to the design, just give us, in your own words, what you did as you proceeded.

A. I selected a colour scheme for my picture, I wanted to paint a warm picture in this instance. I had no psychological reason actually. I just wanted to show a man in a warm night light setting, and I wanted to work in the sculptural setting – a light figure in a dark setting – so I built it up as a sculptor builds up any form; I glazed my colours on to it. Had I used a dark colour or a blue suit for instance, or a dark brown suit, it would have destroyed my form and my design. It would have made just a single head in the centre of the picture and would have lost my effect of light. That is the reason for the light colour.

Q. Do you attach considerable importance to the colour effects in a portrait?

A. I think colour is very important to a painter of portraits.

Q. To what extent did you endeavour to obtain a resemblance to the physical appearance of Mr Smith?

A. I think that was my whole job – ninety per cent of my job, as well as producing a work of art. I think I did get a likeness of Joshua.

Q. In portrait painting, to what extent is there any process of selection or elimination of what you see when you look at the sitter?

A. In all art work it fails if you do not select your design.

Q. What particular influences are manifested in your painting?

A. My particular love is Rembrandt. I studied his methods in Holland and in London. I have had a close acquaintance with them – not copying his brush strokes or his technique, or anything like that, but his aims.

Q. We have heard various expressions of opinion put forward as to how you would judge your own work. Is it modern work or academic in your opinion?

A. I would say classic tradition. I do not like the word academic as applied to a great artist like Rembrandt.

Q. But in one of the London art journals you are described as an academic worker – in the *Art News*, an American publication, in 1941.

A. Yes, I was not called a modernist until I came to Australia.

In London I was regarded amongst artists, and art students, as academic.

Q. And I take it that you do not regard yourself as a modernist?

A. No, definitely.

Mr Barwick then proceeded to the cross-examination.

Q. You say that the elongation or the exaggeration of the arms is also part of that design?

A. Yes, and to stress the elongation of the arms you will notice that I have tightened the sleeves, so that probably you could get a tailor along here to criticize that too. But I tightened the sleeves to give a further impression of the elongation of those arms. You will notice that the arms are not unduly long; it is the tightening of the sleeves that gives that effect.

Q. The arms are very thin.

A. Yes, and the model is very thin; extremely thin.

Q. So that the diminution of the diameter of the arms and the tightening of the clothes and such exaggeration of the length of the arms as is present, are all part of that design of which you speak?

A. Yes, of the picture as a whole.

Q. They are not related to the portrayal of character?

A. Yes, they are all part, naturally –

Q. They are all part of the picture I mean?

A. The character of the physical man, not just his face.

Q. But if you painted him as he actually is, he was thin enough to see that he was thin without exaggeration, wasn't he?

A. Well, you may have noticed that some very thin people wear very loosely made clothes to hide that effect, and loose, wide trousers.

Q. And you have him with loose, wide trousers?

A. Yes, and that is another thing. With those loose, wide trousers one leg hides the other leg, and I did not paint that because I did not see it, any more than I did not paint the hairs on his chest.

Q. Any elongation that took place in the tightening of the sleeves had to do with design, as distinct from the portrayal of character in the picture?

A. It is difficult in two minutes to give lessons on design.

Mr Barwick then proceeded to analyse the portrait piece by piece.

Q. What about the shape of the head, objectively faithful?

A. Yes, I do.

Q. The nose?

A. Yes.

Q. The length of the neck?

A. That I will admit is elongated; the whole thing, you are taking it bit by bit and I am taking it as a picture. I might just as well criticize the conduct of your case by the angle of your wig, as for you to take individual things like that.

It was suggested that the painting was conceived as a jest and only entered for the Archibald Prize at the last moment. Even Dobell's eyesight was questioned.

Q. There is no question of your own capacity in vision, it is not a case of, as I sometimes understand it is with painters, that they cannot see too well?

A. As a matter of fact I have extremely good eyesight.

Ironically, Dobell's eyesight was to become impaired shortly after this as a direct result of the court case.

Q. As he sat before you did he physically appear to your eyes as he appears now on that canvas?

A. On what occasion?

Q. On any occasion?

A. He sat many times.

Q. I don't care if he sat fifty times, did he on any time sitting before you appear to your eyes physically as he appears on that canvas now?

A. It is not necessary –

Q. I did not ask you that, I asked you did he?

A. Yes, within those limits that I have already mentioned. You cannot answer a question like that yes or no, not on an artistic point of art.

Q. Leave the art out for the moment.

A. You cannot leave art out.

Mr Dwyer asked that the witness be treated with elementary fairness; His Honour said that the witness had answered that you could not leave art out.

Later:

Q. You have endeavoured to portray certain aspects of his character?

A. I have portrayed them.

Q. Of course you will agree that in Mr Smith's face there are many more qualities than the characteristics, if they are there at all, assume it for the moment, that you have attempted to portray in the picture?

A. I don't hope to be genius enough to put everything in.

Q. If you painted a more representative picture of his face and set the head in its customary carriage you would convey the idea of stubbornness?

A. I suppose you would. I have not gone far from the representational view as far as I can see.

Q. Leave that for others for the moment, but if you painted a portrait of his face, the whole face in a representational way, and gave it its customary carriage, you would portray stubbornness, is that what you tell us?

A. Would you repeat that?

Q. If you painted his face in a representational way, if you like, a traditional way?

A. What is the traditional way?

Q. If you prefer, in the way in which the professional portraitists paint a face?

A. I am painting in tradition.

Q. You do not regard this in the line of traditional portraiture?

A. You may not think it, I do.

Q. You do not agree with the many witnesses here who put the explanation of this picture on grounds other than traditional portraiture?

A. I certainly do not agree with them.

The question of motives was then examined.

Q. Is this what you are trying to say, that you decided you would paint (1) your conception of him, of his character?

A. I cannot paint anybody else's conception.

Q. Your conception of his character, that you would do that within a given design, and that, subject to those two things, you would seek to make the resultant picture resemble him, is that right?

A. Who gives me the design?

Q. Your design that you used. That you decided (1) on a design (2) that you are going to portray your view of his character?

A. I would not say (1). I used the words 'a conglomeration of all these things'. I did not put anything first.

It was twelve days before Mr Justice Roper announced his judgement. Meanwhile the hearing had aroused popular interest throughout the country. Through the Press it had been given the widest publicity. Probably for the first time an artistic issue had caught the attention of the general public; Dobell's name was on everyone's lips. People who had never been to an art exhibition in their lives eagerly took sides, but those who were involved in the artistic life of the community realized that the case itself was, in effect, a trial of strength between the forces of conservatism and modernism. To those so involved it seemed as though the future hinged on this particular decision, and in the long run this proved to be true. Since then the anti-modernists have been a declining force in Australian art and the modern movement has gone from strength to strength.

On the 8 November the judgement was announced. The Judge began by establishing the nature of the suit, the terms of the will, and the responsibilities of the Trustees in carrying out the intentions of the will that brought the Archibald Prize into existence.

'The question of which among a group of portraits painted by competent artists is the best will always be answered according to the individual tastes and propensities of the observer to whom it is directed. On such a question it would, I think, be safer to expect differences of opinion than to expect unanimity even among persons well qualified by training and experience to give a weighty opinion. In the course of many competitions which have been held for the prize provided by this will, there must, I think, have been frequent occasions when some well-informed body of trained artistic opinion regarded one or more of the entries as being better than that chosen for the award.

'If then a suit were brought in which it was sought to control the administration of the Trust on the grounds that the Trustees' decision as to which of a number of pictures admittedly portraits was the best, it is reasonable to expect that expert evidence could be found to support the view that the choice of the Trustees was wrong. Yet with all his ability and facility of argument Counsel for the relators and the informant was not prepared to argue that such a suit could succeed. In my opinion it could not succeed, without showing *mala fides* on the part of the Trustees, because as a matter of construction of the will the ultimate right of choice is given to the Trustees and as a matter of law where the manner of execution of a trust depends upon the formation by the Trustees of an opinion or the exercise of a judgement this Court will not interfere with its execution unless it is shown that no *bona fide* opinion was formed nor *bona fide* judgement exercised.

'In this suit the award has been canvassed not upon the ground that the picture in respect of which it was made was not the best portrait, but upon the ground that it was not a portrait at all. In my opinion, however, the question whether any competing picture is a portrait is as much a matter upon which the judgement of the Trustees is invoked as is that of whether it is the best portrait. At this stage, however, I should say that the answer to that question depends on the formation of opinions by the observer to whom it is propounded. I think, too, that the testator in this case has submitted that question to the Trustees of the Art Gallery for decision just as he has required them to decide which among competing entries is the best portrait. The same principles of law apply to the decision of the Trustees on each of these questions and in my view the decision of the Trustees that a particular picture is qualified to enter into the competition as being a portrait, is only open to attack upon the grounds that it is not a *bona fide* decision and the onus of establishing the want of *bona fides* is upon the party alleging it.

'It is not alleged in the pleadings nor was it sought to be proved, in this suit, that the decision of the Trustees of the Art Gallery that the picture in respect of which they awarded the prize is a portrait, was a fraudulent decision, in the sense that the Trustees deliberately departed from the terms of the Trust and did not themselves believe that the exhibit was a portrait. In these circumstances I think that before this Court should interfere in the administration of the Trust it must be satisfied that as a matter of objective fact and not of mere opinion the picture is not a portrait, so that the opinion formed by the Trustees to the contrary is founded upon a wrong basis of fact and is not truly an opinion upon the question to which the minds of the Trustees should have been directed.

'If this is the proper test, as I think it is, it is not necessary to interpret the word "portrait" in order to come to the conclusion that the suit fails; because the evidence is overwhelming, in my opinion, that at least there is a proper basis for forming an intelligent opinion that the picture in question is a portrait.

'In view of the manner in which this case was conducted, however, it would not be proper to base a decree merely upon this ground and I proceed to consider the matters to which most of the evidence and argument were directed, namely the interpretation of the word portrait and its application to the picture in question.

'The word is used in a will which was made in 1916 and came into operation in 1919. In my opinion on the evidence there has been no change in its meaning up to the present time. Having heard the evidence of eight persons all highly qualified to express an opinion on the meaning of the word as it is understood by artists, I am satisfied that it has not among

142

artists a technical meaning different from its meaning as an ordinary English word in current use among laymen. Even if it had been found that it had such a technical meaning, it has not been shown that the testator was a member of the class which uses the word in the technical sense. The word is an ordinary word of the English language and its meaning has to be ascertained accordingly.

'With the assistance of dictionaries and the many works to which I have been referred by Counsel in this case, I think that the word "portrait" as used in this will, incorporating in its meaning the limitations imposed by its context, means a pictorial representation of a person, painted by an artist. This definition connotes that some degree of likeness is essential and for the purpose of achieving it the inclusion of the face of the subject is desirable and perhaps essential.

'The picture in question is characterized by some startling exaggerations and distortions clearly intended by the artist, his technique being too brilliant to admit of any other conclusion. It bears, nevertheless, a strong degree of likeness to the subject and is, I think, undoubtedly, a pictorial representation of him. I find as a fact that it is a portrait, within the meaning of the word in this will and consequently the Trustees did not err in admitting it to the competition.

'Whether as a work of art or a portrait, it is good or bad and whether limits of good taste imposed by the relationship of artist and sitter have been exceeded, are questions which I am not called upon to decide and as the expression of my opinion on them could serve no useful purpose I refrain from expressing them. I mention those matters, however, because I think that the witnesses for the informant, whose competency to express opinions in the realm of art is very great, were led into expressing their opinions that the work was not a portrait because they held strong views against it upon those questions. They excluded the work from portraiture, in my opinion, because they have come to regard as essential to a portrait, characteristics which, on a proper analysis of their opinions, are really only essential to what they consider to be good portraiture.

'Finally, I think that it is necessary to state my opinion on the claim that the picture cannot be included as a portrait because it is proper to classify it in another realm of art or work – a caricature according to the information or as fantasy according to a witness for the informant. It is, I think, unnecessary to consider whether the picture could be properly classed as a caricature or fantasy. If it could be so classed that would only establish to my mind that the fields are not mutually exclusive because in my opinion it is in any event properly classed as a portrait. In the result I think that this suit must be dismissed.'

79 *The Berry Pickers, 1947*

CHAPTER FIVE

Wangi: 1945–1949

Dobell's own words describe his reactions to the *Joshua Smith* award and its aftermath. 'I was apprehensive even when I won it. Everything started to happen so quickly. First Joshua's reaction – he congratulated me when I painted it – he loved it at first, but then it won the prize and offended his parents so much that he hasn't spoken to me since. They [the parents] arrived one morning about 7.30 – no, earlier than that because I wasn't out of bed. They wept all over the flat. Being a poor housekeeper I had no handkerchiefs to offer them, so I got a towel. They were handling this wet towel and washing their eyes, begging me never to exhibit it again.'

They offered to buy the portrait of their son but Dobell would not sell it, fearing that it might be destroyed. Finally he said: 'Look, I won't exhibit it again providing you don't publish the fact that I'm not going to exhibit. It will look as though I am ashamed of it! They went straight to the newspapers and gave them the story, so I thought "that lets me out" and I was rather glad. I did exhibit it again.'

This scene occurred on the morning following the award.

As the court case was pending Dobell became a public figure: 'I couldn't go anywhere without being pointed out. I remember all the tram stood up once to look at me. Someone said "Oh, there's Dobell in there" and the whole tram stood up. I hopped out at the next stop and went for my life, trying to bury myself in the crowd. Even at Wangi I couldn't get away from people. I used to hide behind the hedge and they used to come around saying "This is where the mad artist lives" and I would get visitors all around, and holiday-makers watching.'

This, and the strain of the court case, was purgatory for one of Dobell's sensitive and retiring disposition. He withdrew

more and more to the relative peace of Wangi, but his nerve
were shattered. His skin developed a terrible dermatitis from
head to foot, and for a while he lost the use of his left leg. '
used to have to tie it up with a strap and buckle it tight to sto
the pain.'

The dermatitis damaged the left eye. It is still partly blind.

'The skin peeled off me every morning. My sister used to ge
a fire shovel full of skin each morning out of my bed. My
fingers came off like finger stalls, like a cicada loses its skin
almost a complete finger, and my toes like that. My nerve
felt all right during that period, but immediately I was cured
my nerves went to the pack. I was afraid to get up off a chair
and walk outside. Then a woman whose brother-in-law had
been hanged for murder, and who had had a bad nervous
breakdown, she came and told me to take olive oil. I did, and in
about a month I was on my feet walking around and my nerve
were getting stronger. I'm always telling people: "If you have
got somebody going mad tell them to take olive oil. It i
marvellous for the nerves."'

Dobell won the Archibald Award, and his right to it was
vindicated in a court of law, but his was the sort of victory that
no one can afford to win. It costs too much. Misfortune seems
to have singled out this portrait for its own. Some years later
it was bought by Mr E. W. Hayward (later Sir William Hayward) of Adelaide, and was damaged beyond hope of restora-
tion by a fire that swept through the library on the night of
Sunday, 1 June 1958.

The house Dobell came to live in at Wangi had been built
by his father as a holiday home. It stands on the foreshore of
Lake Macquarie looking north. Later additions have given it
the atmosphere of a spacious Mediterranean villa. A sunny
terrace is shaded by a high Jacaranda tree and across the foot-
path that separates the house from the water's edge is a line
of graceful casuarinas. Only in the summer months, especially
during the school holidays, do campers and trippers destroy
the tranquillity of the scene. Sometimes a westerly will raise a

146

rop of white caps on the lake and more rarely a black nor'-aster will come howling in with the smell of the tropics on s breath. Generally it is peaceful and it was peace that Dobell eeded after the turmoil. During his long illness he was looked fter by his sister, Alice.

Gradually he became interested in painting again. It was the andscape at Wangi that started him working once more. He vould sit on the veranda and make little gouache studies of the cene before him. At first he thought little enough of them. 'hey were exercises to keep his hand in. Then the mood of he place began to take hold of him and in the next few years le made dozens of sketches and a number of beautiful and ully developed paintings. Of these, the three most satisfying re *The Narrows Beach*, *The Westerly Breeze*, and the justifiably amous *Storm Approaching Wangi* which won the Wynne Prize or landscape in 1948. He also won his second Archibald Prize vith his portrait of Margaret Olley, the following year.

Ills. 80, 82, 83

Ill. 90

o *The Narrows Beach, second version, 1956*

The Narrows Beach was the first of his Australian landscape to be publicly exhibited. The artist borrowed it back from Mrs Thelma Clune to exhibit at the 1948 Exhibition of th Society of Artists. On the 4 September it was stolen from th Education Department's Art Gallery and has never been recovered.

Ill. 80 Some years later Dobell painted a second version for Mr Clune and although there are slight differences in detail, it i substantially the same as the stolen painting.

His paintings seem to attract the attention of art thieves Earlier, in 1942, his *Study for a Woman Dozing* disappeared from the Art Gallery of New South Wales. Again in 1949 anothe small painting *The Guitar Player* was stolen from its owne Mr Eugene Ormandy in the United States, and only a few years ago *The Little Milliner* was taken from the Art Gallery but returned anonymously some months afterwards.

Strangely enough, the paintings he now began to produce a Wangi showed very little sign of the stresses and strains he had been through. The landscapes of these years were so fresh and sparkling that one could believe the artist had not a single car in the world.

Ill. 81 The earliest of the post-Joshua portraits, *Thelma Clune* shows an unusual tension in its colour scheme. A conflict o reds and greens produces an effect of animation that has . nervous edge to it, but the period culminates in the 194? *Ill. 90* portrait of Margaret Olley the most sumptuously blooming of all his portraits.

By the end of 1945 Dobell was back in his stride again, bu there was a subtle difference in the work he now produced Consciously, or unconsciously, he turned away from the mor extreme forms of his earlier work. Jibes, such as the on describing the *Joshua Smith* as a portrait of a seasick skeleton had had a devastating effect on him. His sense of purpose had been shaken; he was no longer sure that he was heading in th right direction. Up till the time of the débâcle he had neve doubted that what he was doing was what he should be doing

81
Thelma Clune,
1945

He had painted the way he did because it was natural for him
to paint that way. Now he'd been brought up with a jolt. A
lot of people thought he was wrong, and although he consciously rejected their criticisms as invalid because they were
born of ignorance or misunderstanding, he was none the less
shocked by the bitterness his work provoked.

Whether he deliberately tried to avoid provocation in his
new paintings, or whether it was an instinctive reaction of
self-defence would be difficult to say. Once, in the portrait of
restaurateur, Walter Magnus, called *Chez Walter* he gives   *Ill. 84*
notice that he can still use the most vehement methods when he
feels the occasion demands it.

But generally, his choice of subjects and his treatment o them indicated an inclination to avoid contention and dispute

No one could quarrel with his landscapes – unless they trie to identify the spot it purports to record; as we have alread mentioned, Dobell the landscapist, rarely works *en plein ai* At most he will set down a brief note from the subject befor him, but more often than not he will simply commit a scen to memory and make a sketch of it when he returns home.

When he went to Hong Kong in 1961 he did not keep diary, but each night, in a sketchbook, he would sum up th impressions of the day in page after page of drawings done a lightning speed from images still vividly alive in his mind' eye. This sketch-book is a quarry from which he still works

The Wangi landscapes will only baffle those who think a artist's job is to produce hand-made photographs. It would b hard to identify a single spot from his finished landscapes despite their air of verisimilitude. They are truer to the spiri of the place than to any single aspect of it. Yet, they are un mistakably of Wangi.

Such an approach is entirely different to that of the Impres sionists, though his landscapes often resemble those of th Impressionist masters, and of Renoir in particular. Dobel almost invariably painted in the studio from sketches an memories; most of the Impressionists painted on the spot an only for as long as the light was constant. When they becam conscious of a change in the light they stopped painting, an would not return until another day provided identical con ditions. Dobell has too little of the scientist in him to becom absorbed in the study of light and in the problem of duplicating its qualities in pigment. To him it was more important to catc the spirit of the place than to define the exact nature of th atmosphere that enveloped it, more important to express hi feelings about the place than to describe it objectively an precisely in terms of light sensations.

Certainly, his landscapes are flooded with light of variou kinds – he was too keen an observer not to have noticed th effect light and air produce – but the light is characteristic rather than particular. He describes a kind of day rather than a specific hour of a specific day, and he prefers those days when movements in the air stir the leaves and the water into a tremulous catch and loss of light till the atmosphere seems alive with tiny sparks of pale fire.

Of the three 1948 landscapes *The Narrows Beach* is the most *Ill. 80* classical in its composition, and the most nearly classical in spirit.

When it comes to painting people Dobell never idealizes in the spirit of the classical masters. He may sometimes generalize, but if he does so it is not because he wants to perfect imperfections, eliminate incongruities, or correct the mistakes of nature, but because he wants to establish the individual as a symbol for a particular type of human being. This kind of generalization leads him to underline the very characteristics that vary from the norm – the opposite process to that of Michelangelo or Raphael. Even if we can sometimes look at a Dobell and think of the image as a symbol of gluttony, arrogance, shrewdness, energy, or bitterness, we still think of them as individuals whose characteristics are strongly developed in a specific direction. They are never merely masks for an abstract conception.

In a few landscapes he allows himself the luxury of idealization.

The Narrows Beach has something of the strictness of Poussin in its organization, though its colour suggests the healthy sensuousness of Renoir. A corrugated-iron boat-shed has been given the proportions and volume of a Greek temple, the curves of the beached rowing boat in the foreground are echoed in the curve of a tree-trunk or the line of a distant hill, yet any suggestion of formality is counteracted by the animation of the surface.

Most poetic of all his landscapes is *The Westerly Breeze*. Here *Ill. 82* the composition is much less static. Slender tree-trunks break across the boldly curving shore-line at irregular intervals. It is a landscape full of subtle rhythms moving in a milky light. His colour has never before been so deliciously tremulous and elusive.

Most dramatic of all his 1948 landscapes is *Storm Approaching* Ill. 83 *Wangi*. Figures play a more important part in this painting. Our eyes are caught by the woman's alert attention as the two men struggle to bring the boat through the wind-whipped shallows, but the real drama is in the coming storm. Already the wind has blurred the needles of the casuarina into clouds as dark as those of the nearing storm centre. The tree-trunks snake down through the disturbed air like black lightning. Over on the far side of the lake the water is sombre and still because the hills still protect it from the wind. An ominous light flickers among the trees and there is the rumble of thunder in the air.

82 *The Westerly Breeze, 1948*

83 Storm Approaching Wangi, 1948

True to his love of paradox Dobell has made this his whitest
painting – a symphony in silver. Where almost any other artist
would have darkened his palette to suit the subject, Dobell
has gone to the other extreme and lightened his to an extraordinary degree. The surface is coated with a thick impasto of
white, and the touch varies from the abrupt ripple and chop of
the waves to the coiling boil of the thunder-heads filling the sky.

These were not the only landscapes of the period, and he was
to continue with Wangi subjects for many years to come, but
these three are his most fully developed statements about his
surroundings at Wangi. His later landscapes had a completely
different character.

Perhaps the most spectacular, and certainly the most unusual
of his portraits between the court case and *Margaret Olley*, is
Chez Walter. As its name implies, it is not simply a portrait of   *Ill. 84*
Walter Magnus. A search for a likely prototype would probably
take us back to Watteau's miraculous *L'Enseigne de Gersaint*,
for this, too, is a kind of glorified shop sign. It tells us not only

153

what Walter Magnus looked like and what sort of a person he was, but what he did for a living. It is at once a portrait and an advertisement.

The bulky figure of the gourmet restaurateur is set, like a moon nearing its full splendour, in a design of Rococo delicacy. What other painter, faced with such a massive subject, would think of presenting it as a ruby-red fantasy of curving scrolls as exquisitely playful as the decoration of the Amalienburg? Here is another example of Dobell's contra-suggestibility. Given a more than ordinarily heavy figure of a man to paint, Dobell's quirkish imagination persuaded him to present the subject in terms of its opposite characteristic. He seemed to delight in making things difficult for himself; in setting himself a seemingly insoluble problem and finding a satisfactory answer for it.

84 Chez Walter, 1945

*85 Flying Officer
James Bullmore, 1946*

To paint a heavy man heavily would be too cut and dried a response. So he complicates the issue by painting his heaviness with the lightest of touches and the most graceful of gestures. He gives us a portrait of a man who is an artist with food – a man who can create as delicately for the palate as Cuvilliés created for the eye in the rooms of the Amalienburg. The portraits of Thelma Clune, Frank Clune, and Professor L.F.Giblin are much more straightforward. Each is a brilliantly observed character study, but as works of art they break no new ground.

Whatever he did Dobell could be relied upon to achieve a stylish result. In 1946 he painted the portrait of Flying Officer James Bullmore from photographs. Flying Officer Bullmore *Ill. 85* had been killed on active service in New Guinea, but it would be difficult to guess from the painting that the airman had not actually posed for the artist. It is full of the kind of observation

155

86 *Boy with a Dog, 1949*

normally acquired only by direct experience. By comparison,

Ill. 87 the portrait of Miss Marcia Moses in *The White Lace Dress* seems much less 'alive'. It is an amazing *tour de force*, but one is inclined to remember the dress rather than the face – a circumstance the artist must have been aware of, since he did not call it a portrait.

One of the most charming works of this period is the small

Ill. 86 *Boy with a Dog* now in the National Gallery of Victoria.

Swiftly, yet subtly painted, it brings to mind some of the London paintings, though the colour is stronger and more dramatic and the mood more romantic. The young fair-haired boy is standing with his arms behind his head – the way children sometimes do when they don't quite know what to do with themselves.

87 *The White Lace Dress, 1946*

88 Pencil Study for Margaret Olley, 1948

Perhaps he has been called in to go to bed, since it is quite dark. But he doesn't want to go to bed and would rather play with the little dog. There is just a suggestion of defiance in the way he stands, and a feeling that he is waiting for a parent to make the next move.

At the end of 1948 Dobell won his second Archibald Prize *Ill. 90* with the portrait of fellow artist *Margaret Olley* and there can

89 Sketch for Margaret Olley, 1948

be no doubt that it must rank among the finest things he has
ever done.

It is a portrait in the grand manner. The young artist sits
sideways in a high-back Victorian arm-chair. On her left there
is a table with a bowl of fruit, and behind it a mirror reflecting
the back of her large flower-decked hat. Like *Elaine Haxton*, she
seems to be ready for a garden-party, in a dress of palest green

Ill. 67

with a scarf of lilac silk. Overtones of eighteenth-century elegance are blended with a warm serenity that would have appealed to Renoir who, of all artists, loved to paint 'a skin that takes the light'; Dobell has flooded his sitter in a summer radiance.

In Greece there are limestone paths that countless feet have polished into pewter mirrors. The Greek light strikes upwards from them till you believe they are the actual source of light. You walk on a path of diamond fire.

Margaret Olley creates a similar illusion. The paint seems actually incandescent. Of all his portraits it is the most radiant, the most delightful, the most engaging.

Unlike Renoir, who only enjoyed painting beautiful things, Dobell could be happy with subjects not usually regarded as beautiful in themselves. He did not need the stimulus of physical beauty as a necessary spur to creation. He could create beauty from the ugly, the sordid, or the ridiculous, for he realized that a thing that is ugly in nature can be transformed by the artist's vision into a thing of beauty. Natural and aesthetic beauty are not synonymous terms. A gorgeous sunset does not necessarily make a satisfying painting, while a rape, a murder, or an execution can sometimes inspire the highest art.

Rembrandt went to an *abattoir* and returned with a majestic painting. Brueghel and Goya could even salvage something of aesthetic value from the horrors of war; and Dobell could look at the seamiest scenes and transmute their dross into the precious metal of art.

Yet Dobell is not afflicted with the kind of malignant puritanism that prevents him from relishing beauty simply because it is beautiful. He does not mistrust beauty, and for him it is only one aspect of the fact of living, no more or no less important than the aspects conventionally excluded as unsuitable for art.

When he has a chance to paint a Renoiresque subject he rises to the occasion in a magnificent manner.

90 *Margaret Olley, 1948*

91 Mount William, Nondugl, 1951

92 Wahgi Valley, Nondugl, 1949

CHAPTER SIX

The New Guinea Paintings: 1949–1953

For Dobell a desert is a desert; it is not a soul-expanding antechamber to eternity, where revelations shape and reshape themselves in hot dry air like mirages; nor is it a breeding-ground for myths. His eyes discover no especial beauty in its barrenness, and besides, it is too underpopulated to appeal to an artist whose main interest is in people. The Dead Heart of the Continent means nothing to Dobell. He has no curiosity about it, and if he saw it he would not want to paint it for he is, in truth, an urban painter. There are two remarkable exceptions to his urban interests – the Wangi landscapes and the unique series of paintings he made of New Guinea subjects. Even so, the earlier Wangi paintings express a city-man's view of the countryside. They emphasize its picturesqueness and its charm, but they do not probe into the bush's secrets with the searching stare of a dedicated bush painter like Clifton Pugh.

Dobell makes no attempt to understand the impersonal cruelties and the harsh necessities that govern existence in the bushland. For him the landscape is merely an extension of his own personality, a mirror of his own moods – it is tranquil, gently stirring, or stormy, but it is tamed and organized like a landscape garden.

If this is interpreted as a superficial approach then we must regard most of the great landscape paintings of history as superficial, for Dobell began his landscape painting on the basis of a long tradition. As we shall see, his later landscapes and beach scenes branch away in a new direction, but he has never shown any interest in what might be described as the 'post-Darwinian' approach.

In Australia, the chief protagonist of this kind of landscape painting is undoubtedly Clifton Pugh. He sees the bush as a laboratory in which nature demonstrates her methods, or as a battleground in which the struggle for survival is continuously enacted.

Perhaps the nearest Dobell ever came to this type of painting was in his *Fighting Bulls* painted in 1959. Not only is the subject unique among his works, but he has set it against a landscape of appropriate starkness that is much more characteristic of the country than it is of Dobell's art.

The other exception is more genuinely an exception. Nothing prepared us for the New Guinea paintings and they remain embedded in the volume of his work as brilliant exotics.

Shortly after Easter in 1949 Sir Edward Hallstrom chartered a plane to fly a group of guests to his experimental sheep station at Nondugl in the highlands of Central New Guinea. Among these guests were Senator Armstrong, writer Frank Clune and his wife, writer Colin Simpson, and artist William Dobell.

93 *Sketch for The Orchid Gatherers, 1949*

94 Mathias, 1953

Dobell was fascinated by what he saw. Vivid tropical greens, red earth, strong blue skies, the dark bodies of the natives with faces sometimes painted like masks, or enveloped in a fantasy of Bird-of-Paradise plumes – these provoked him into an immediate outburst of water-colour painting and sketching. But such things were not easy to set down without making them look like posters for a tropical cruise. When he looked at his efforts again after a few days he destroyed the lot and started all over again.

During the next two months Dobell learnt to see the landscape and its inhabitants in a new way. Wherever he went he drew and painted, mostly in water-colour.

95 (above left)
Study for Women
setting the Table,
Nondugl, 1951

96 (centre left)
Early version of
The Thatchers, 1950

97 (below left)
Sketch for Love
Song, 1950

98 Frandam, 1953

99 Workshop, Nondugl, 1951

Back at Wangi he began to develop his sketches into oil paintings. He was haunted by the strangeness of New Guinea, for he was aware of a sense of primitive mystery shrouding the land as palpably as clouds banked on high places. For months he worked to express his experiences but in April 1950 he felt obliged to go back – to check and expand his impressions.

This time he stayed at Government House, Port Moresby, as a guest of the Administrator, before setting out to revisit Nondugl, Mount Hagen, and the Wahgi Valley area. Later he extended his travels to include the Sepik River area. He did some delightful sketches at Angoram, and went for several hundred miles up the river on a launch carrying supplies to outposts in the interior.

From his first visit in 1949 until the beginning of 1954 when he was persuaded to exhibit his recent work in Sydney, Dobell painted little else but New Guinea subjects. All these paintings were small and some of the finest of them would almost qualify as miniatures. Working from sketches made on the spot, and aided by his phenomenal visual memory, the artist painted a succession of tiny masterpieces of such exquisite delicacy that one is constantly being reminded of Watteau. Not that any of them look remotely like a Watteau, but they have the same knack of achieving strength by the most delicate means.

Gauguin is the artist who immediately comes to mind when we think of natives in a tropical setting, but Dobell refused to look in his direction. Though he was fascinated by the intense colour of the landscape, and by the way dark skins can take and hold every sort of light, these things could never be as central to Dobell's art as they were to the art of Gauguin. For him a native is a person rather than a pattern. Most of the people in Gauguin's Tahitian paintings look alike; none of them are stamped with the characteristics of a unique personality. After all, Gauguin had other fish to fry; he was never very interested in other people.

Decorative generalizations make little appeal to Dobell and he has given us a series of actual portraits of natives. *Frandam,*

Ill. 98

168

100 Boy in a
White Lap Lap, 1952

Mathias, the *Boy in a White Lap Lap*, the *Kuta Girl*, and the
Boy with Bow are real people.

Ills. 94,
100, 111

Frandam could be a younger, more civilized sister of the
'Kuta Girl'. Both wear expressions of wistful melancholy but
the older girl is still in her tribal finery, while young Frandam
has exchanged her shell ornaments for a European-type dress.
Burly, confident Mathias, with his name tattooed across his
chest is a complete contrast to the shy, coltish angularity of the
boy with the bow and arrow. Mathias is used to white men and
their ways. So, too, is the boy in the white lap lap for he is, in
all probability, a servant in a white man's house. But the boy

with the bow and arrow may never have been in such a house, and has probably seen only a few white men in his life. Though he is posed with natural grace, there is a sense of wariness in the way he holds the arrow, even though his left hand has relaxed on the bow.

As in his London work, Dobell's New Guinea paintings fall into three categories – portraits, genre paintings, and landscapes.

One of the most fascinating of the genre paintings is called *Kanana* and Colin Simpson, who was with Dobell in New Guinea, has given us a description of a kanana (probably the same one Dobell painted) in his book *Plumes and Arrows* (Angus & Robertson 1962).

Ill. 103

'. . . a long low house had been built of cane and kunai – it was about eighty feet long. Right down the middle of this a line of fires had been lighted in shallow holes scraped in the earth floor. The couples were seated between these small fires down the length of the hut.

'When I came stooping in through the one door, it seemed incredible that so many people could bear to be enclosed with as much smoke as there was in this chimneyless, windowless place with its roof so low that I could not stand upright.'

Simpson had with him a tape recorder, and proceeded to record his impressions.

'What are they doing? They're rolling their faces together, turning their heads to the rhythm of the singing, forehead against forehead, cheek against cheek so that their lips almost touch, and with this motion their torsos sway from side to side. Their eyes are closed and from their lips comes a low throaty singing that sometimes falls away into humming and never rises into stridency. The refrain you could almost call "haunting" and it is as sensuous as a love-song should be. For the refrain there are, I am told, no words, but the verses of the songs they sing have mainly to do with birds and trees and places, the things of nature the native lives so close to.

'These kananas continue into the morning hours. Usually there is a married woman present, a matron who acts as a

101 *Sketch for Girls under Pandanus Tree, 1949*

102 *Natives Carrying a Pig, 1950*

103 Kanana, 1950

mistress of ceremonies, and from time to time she will tell the couples to change partners. However, a girl may decline to kanana with a man she does not like, or she may go through the movements only as a polite formality; if she participates with intensity the man knows that she likes him. At some kananas there is a stage when all the men leave and then certain favoured ones are invited, through the matron, to return. When this happens and the fires die down, the couples may move and sit against the wall and there they will, in the pidgin term, "carry leg". The girl puts her legs over and between the legs of the man. In this position the couple can still, to an extent, carry on the "turnim head", but it becomes what we call "petting" and some love-play is often associated with it, and it may lead to intercourse when the fires die out, though by that time, I am told, couples who have kananaed all through the night are mostly too tired to do anything but sleep. It depends too on the vigilance of the supervision, as well as on how erotically

172

inclined the couples feel. The purpose of the kanana is not to sanction promiscuity but to provide opportunity for man and girl to "get to know each other"; but there seems to be more tolerance of them doing this sexually than there is in our society.'

Dobell has painted the kanana while the fires are still brightly burning, but for the sake of pictorial simplicity he has sliced away one half of the building so that it looks like a pavilion with one side open to the night. There is still a green glimmer

104 *The Thatchers, 1953*

of light on the horizon, but night has darkened the upper reaches into indigo and the air is alive with fire-flies.

Characteristically Dobellian is the decision to present this most sensuous of subjects in a composition of the strictest formality. Nothing could be more severe than the geometry of this little painting. It almost seems to be a rule with Dobell that the firmness of the design works in a direct ratio to the emotional content of the subject; those most fraught with emotion are subjected to the most rigorous treatment.

Here there is a rigidity in the placement of forms that Mondrian would surely have appreciated. The whole scene is presented in uncompromising frontality. Divisions and subdivisions are precisely calculated, intervals are exquisitely judged, and the figures themselves have been resolved into a series of entwining arabesques, a calligraphy of fire-glazed lines against a warm darkness.

105 Boy with a Parakeet, 1952

06 Fishing Nets at Koki Beach, 1955

By so doing Dobell has emphasized the ritualistic element
in the ceremony. He has not seen the kanana merely as the
local equivalent of a Saturday night teenage dance, or a socially
sanctioned petting party. He has transformed it into a mystical
rite. He has cleansed the air of eye-stinging smoke and filled it
with fire-flies; the three smokeless fires spring magically from
the earth, and the faces are so painted that they resemble masks
rather than human features. By the symmetry of the grouping
he has created a suggestion of ceremony. What must have
been a rather earthy spectacle has been transformed by art and
endowed with a mysterious timelessness. They have become
celebrants of the timeless mystery of the flesh.

Elsewhere in Simpson's book, the writer quotes Dobell as
saying: 'Up there everything seemed to me to take the form
of plumes, to repeat the designs of the feathers the natives

175

decorated themselves with – the bamboos for instance, pluming
up like terrific ostrich feathers in beautiful green, and the little
white torrents coming down the sides of the mountains have
the same lovely romantic movement, and the design comes to
you again in the roll of the wind on the kunai grass.'

Dobell captures the essence of these feathery fuming moun-
tain rapids in *The Torrent* where pale water plumes froth
between dark banks and boulders. This is one of the most
original and captivating of his New Guinea landscapes with
figures, but perhaps the strangest and most magical of them

Ill. 104 all is *The Thatchers*.

No doubt the artist had seen the natives at work thatching
the roofs of their huts and, fascinated by their agile movements,
he made several studies of them. An early version of the subject remains fairly close to the visual experience, but Dobell
could not leave it at that. He wanted to convey the fact that
they were working high in the air above his head.

In the final version he has placed them literally in the sky,
like a troupe of multi-coloured nude and wingless angels.
Curiously, they call to mind the floating angels in Botticelli's
Nativity in the National Gallery, London. It, too, has a thatched
roof in the upper part of the picture, three angels kneel on it,
and above it a circlet of ecstatic angels move weightlessly in
the tranquil air. In Dobell's painting only three slender poles

107 *The Bird Catchers, 1952*

108 *The Bird Watchers, 1953*

remind us that the figures are working on a roof and are not, in fact, an aerial manifestation of supernatural beings. The landscape is bare and deserted like the plains one crosses in dreams. Away in the distance a range of hills divides the picture into upper and lower halves. Contrary to all the normal laws of composition, everything takes place in the upper half; the lower half is featureless except for a suggestion of fallen reeds and the three cursory posts that are far too flimsy to perform their ostensible function. At the top of the picture there is a little white oval cloud, such as one sometimes finds in trecento paintings, with the hand of God issuing from it in benediction. No hand issues from this cloud, but such a hand would not have been inappropriate, for one feels that the labour of making a roof has been given a spiritual significance in this extraordinary painting. Even the ribs of the roof seem to fall from the sky like a symbol of blessing.

If ever form and colour can create in the eye a sense of melody, then this painting sings. No doubt the colour of native skins does vary and Dobell has taken advantage of this fact, but he has so heightened and ordered his colour sequence that the eye moves from figure to figure with a sense of rise and fall comparable to the intervals in a musical theme. The twisting bodies are garlanded across the upper painting in a shallow crescent, but the colours leap up and down the scale with wonderful flexibility.

Colour has always fascinated Dobell. He was never an artist who could regard it as an adjunct to drawing. For him it was an integral part of the creative process, not something to be added after all the other problems had been solved. We have seen how his sensitive eye reacted to his environment. In London his colour tended to be reticent, and at times almost monochromatic, but it never lacked subtlety and it always developed naturally out of the nature of the subject. Australian sunlight caused his colour to blossom in full chromatic brilliance and we have noticed that even the London subjects painted in Sydney were more richly coloured. Sometimes colour would be used in its descriptive capacity, but with increasing frequency Dobell began to use it for its emotional effect. Now, in New Guinea, his colours took on a bejewelled quality, as though keyed to the exotic plumage of the Birds-of-Paradise. He loved to use colours that are not what they seemed, to compose his neutrals by juxtaposing complementary colours. This device he inherited from the Impressionists but he rarely used it, as an Impressionist would, to create a sense of atmosphere. He used it because a neutral thus constructed has the feeling of neutrality, yet a closer inspection excites the eye

178

109 *Rain over the Wahgi, 1949*

with a thousand tiny clashes. It creates a neutrality full of subtle tensions. It makes us conscious of the fact that the neutrality is a precariously held balance of opposing forces.

Many of his later works are built on this principle, but most of his New Guinea paintings wear their jewellery with fewer inhibitions. In *Mahme and Tamba Player* for instance, he delights in the frank yellowness of the woman's body with its painted designs and vermilion face. *Love Song* is indeed sung with languorous colour; *The Bird Catchers*, *The Bird Watchers*, and *Boy with a Parakeet* have colour as lusciously appealing as tropical fruit; it is sonorous and richly orchestrated in the landscape with *Natives Carrying a Pig*, darkly mysterious in the sketch for *Girls Under Pandanus Tree*, gentle and lyrical in the *Fishing Nets at Koki Beach* and the garden-like scene at *Angoram on the Sepik River*; sombre and thunderous in the turbulently painted *Head of Kuta Girl* which Dobell, himself, regards as one of his strongest paintings.

Ill. 110

Ill. 97
Ills. 107,
108, 105

Ill. 102
Ill. 101
Ill. 106

Ill. 111

These and others like them create a unique body of work, for they present a remote and little-known part of the world as seen through the eyes of a major painter.

Hardly less attractive than the finished oil paintings are the dozens of sketches and gouache studies made on the spot, or worked up from even briefer sketches.

Ills. 109, 93 *Rain over the Wahgi* and *The Orchid Gatherers* are beautiful examples of Dobell's keenness of observation and delicacy of touch.

However, these years were not entirely devoted to New Guinea subjects. Between 1950 and 1953 he painted a number of commissioned portraits – *Sir Hudson Fysh* in 1950; *Sir Charles* *Ill. 114* *Lloyd Jones* and *Anthony Quayle as Falstaff* in 1951; *Tony Clune, Professor Hedley Marston*, and *Lady Lloyd Jones* in 1952. Of these the best is undoubtedly the portrait of *Anthony Quayle as*

110 *Mahme and Tamba Player, 1953*

111 *Head of Kuta Girl, 1953*

112 Pilchards, 1953

Falstaff where every brush stroke has the swirling rotundity and bombast of Shakespeare's immortal character. It is a superb example of Dobell, the stylist, placing his style at the service of the character. It is enlightening to bear this portrait in mind

Ill. 115   while studying the later portrait of Dame Mary Gilmore – the contrast between the two manners of painting shows the range of Dobell's command and the extraordinary way he can adjust his style to the character of his sitter.

There were other works as well – the boldly drawn *Goldie*, the engaging little *Wangi Boy*, the vigorously painted *Boy in*

Ill. 112   *Jodhpurs* and the crisply defined *Pilchards* – his first still-life in many years.

113 Portrait of a Cat, 1952

114 *Anthony Quayle as Falstaff, 1951*

115 *Dame Mary Gilmore, 1957*

CHAPTER SEVEN

Later Works: 1954–1968

Though Dobell yielded to persuasion and exhibited his New Guinea work he did so against his better judgement. He regarded most of the exhibited paintings as preliminary essays and planned to spend several more years working from his store of sketches. He felt he was only just beginning to express the feel of the place.

Most of the reviews were laudatory, but the critic of the influential *Sydney Morning Herald* took him to task for having become a miniaturist and for losing the boldness of his earlier paintings. Such a criticism is based on the assumption that the critic knows better than the artist himself what the artist should do. Because he had not painted his pictures in a manner to which we were accustomed, it was easy to regard the newer work as a falling off. Today we can see that the delicacy and the

116 Impression of Hong Kong, 1963

boldness are both equally characteristic of Dobell's art, and to regret one in favour of the other is simply to express a personal preference. Dobell, the artist, is a complex of many different and sometimes opposing qualities. He is the sum of many separate things and to eliminate one of them would be to diminish his stature.

But Dobell has few defences against criticism. The sensitivity that gives his portraits such subtlety and perceptiveness leaves him without much protection. He is made vulnerable by the very traits that make him the kind of artist he is.

As a result of this criticism he abandoned his intention of continuing with the New Guinea subjects, and though he has turned back to them once or twice over the past ten years he has never rekindled the fire of his first enthusiasm.

In recent years he has not been a prolific painter and a serious illness brought his work to a standstill for over a year. In January 1958 he was operated on for cancer and it was not until the beginning of 1959 that he felt well enough to paint again.

He still lives at Wangi with his sister and, as a result of this semi-rural isolation, there have been fewer and fewer genre paintings – and none at all since 1954. He needed the city streets and cafés to prompt him to this kind of painting. But the later period has been rich in fine portraits, and his landscape painting has taken a new direction.

None of the newer landscapes and beach scenes are painted with the degree of finish that marked his early work. His interest now lies in seizing a particular movement and extending it through a range of variations and inversions until the whole painting pulsates with related rhythms. He had already ex-
Ill. 103 plored some of these possibilities in *Kanana*, in which each of the couples is virtually a variation on a single rhythmic theme; but in these later paintings he was to carry the rhythm through to every part of the painting.

His visual imagination can be triggered into action by the most unlikely experience. Once, while casually glancing at a newspaper lying upside-down on the table, he thought he saw

186

a strangely contorted figure in the corner of a photograph. When he turned it round the figure disappeared and the parts he had mistaken for a torso with folded limbs were something else altogether. The mistaken interpretation caught his imagination. Turning the page upside-down again he sketched the shape, giving it his original interpretation and from this germ a series of beach scenes evolved.

At this time he had been commissioned by Her Majesty the Queen, and the Duke of Edinburgh, to paint two pictures for Windsor Castle. Casting round for subjects of a typically Australian character, he finally decided on a *Beach Carnival* and a *Country Race Meeting*. The motif taken from the upside-down newspaper photograph became the leading theme of the *Beach Carnival* and the series of studies that led up to it. What fascinated him most about the crowded beach scene was the spectacle of a dense mass of human bodies united by their allegiance to the sun, the surf, and the sand; to stress their communion he painted the sea, the clouds, the banners, the surfers, and the sunbathers in a twisting complex of rhythms in which the body has little more substance than a cloud or a breeze-twitched banner.

117 Sketch for Galloping Horses, 1960

In 1960 Dobell painted three or four small pictures which he describes as abstracts. They are exquisitely wrought linear fantasies. Perhaps it would be better to call them exercises in free rhythm, for the line moves on the impulse of the moment, building a web of movement that suggests a figure, a butterfly, or a prawn.

They are attractive by-products of Dobell's talents, as are the sketches he has made from the television images of Aneurin Bevan and Joan Sutherland, but the great works of the later

118 Portrait of Helena Rubinstein, 1957

119 *Woman in a Salon, 1960*

period have all been portraits, of which the most magnificent is the *Dame Mary Gilmore*, and the most astonishing the series   *Ill. 115* of eight he has painted of Helena Rubinstein.   *Ills. 118, 119*

As usual the style took its cue from the subject. The *Rock Fisherman* is painted with a brush that surges over the panel like ocean water curling and sweeping among rocks. *Rattails*,   *Ill. 122* painted from a girl he memorized on a bus, is all delicate attenuation and subtle modelling; *Anne Hamer*, all curves and   *Ill. 123* luscious colour, is a complete contrast to the gangling cheeki-ness of *Johnnie Russell* or the brisk decisiveness of *Blair Ritchie*.   *Ill. 120* When he painted the philosopher Professor John Anderson he   *Ill. 125* gave the pose the static dignity one associates with the serenity of wisdom, but within the large clear forms the paint is alive with inquiring rhythms, like a mind constantly on the alert for new ideas, and although the colour creates an illusion of cool, meditative aloofness it is actually based on an opposition of green and violet.

As we shall see when we turn to the Helena Rubinstein paintings, Dobell has a habit of tackling the same theme over and over again.

Ill. 126   The 1962 *Portrait on a Terrace* is not, strictly speaking, a new version of an older subject. He had never before painted a portrait of Bob King, who posed for this painting, but it is
Ill. 84   difficult to avoid linking it with the *Chez Walter* painted seventeen years earlier in 1945. The pose and the stylistic treatment of Walter Magnus and Bob King are closely related, but

120 Johnnie Russell, 1955   *121 Portrait of a Youth, 1954*

122 Rattails, 1959   *123 Anne Hamer, 1955*

Dobell never really repeats himself – the differences are far
more illuminating than the similarities. Magnus sits in the
ruby-red dimness of his domain, while King sits in the cool
sunlight of the artist's terrace. They are as opposite in colour
as paintings can be. Nor does the difference end there. In the
earlier painting, the artist has carried the circling lines of the
figure into every part of the picture. Magnus belongs to his
setting because the artist has made the setting an extension of
the man.

    In the later picture he has made no attempt to do this – in
fact he seems to have gone out of his way to isolate the figure
from its setting, for the feathery delicacy of the landscape is
quite alien to the solidly curving bulk of the sitter. This dis-
crepancy is obviously intentional, for Dobell is an artist of
extreme sensitivity in matters of this sort. He would never
arrive at this kind of result through a failure of his aesthetic

125 *Portrait of Professor John Anderson, 1962*

sensibilities. It is deliberate, and the effect it creates is of a character subtly out of tune with his surroundings. He has run the risk of spoiling the unity of the painting in order to point out a psychological fact, and this courageous honesty makes it a memorable work. In any case he has avoided any danger of real disunity by binding everything together with closely related colour.

In 1959 Dobell won his third Archibald Prize with a portrait of the surgeon who had operated on him two years earlier – Dr E. G. MacMahon. Of his three prize-winning portraits this *Ill. 127* is the most straightforward and direct. Being a Dobell it goes without saying that the likeness will be a good one, in both the visual and psychological sense, and that the paint itself will be lively. It even goes further than that, for the artist tells us something of his own attitude to the surgeon whose skill had

124 *Lydia with Hair in Pins, 1963*

saved his life. Our attention is focused as much on the hands as on the face. The benign expression, the steady gaze, and the strong capable hands are the key to Dobell's attitude. Dressed in an anonymous suit instead of the antiseptic robes of the operating theatre we would probably still place this man as a doctor.

Besides being a portrait of Edward MacMahon it is an icon of a doctor – a symbol of a profession.

Since 1960 Dobell has painted portraits of celebrities for the cover of *Time* Magazine. The first to appear was that of

Ill. 128 Australia's Prime Minister Menzies for the issue of 4 April 1960. For the 4 August issue of 1961 he painted South Viet-Nam's President Ngo Dinh Diem and for the 18 May 1962 cover he painted a portrait of General Motors' Chairman Frederic G. Donner.

The portrait of the Prime Minister, now Sir Robert Menzies, was painted in his studio at Wangi from water-colour sketches he made at two sittings in the Prime Minister's Canberra

126 Portrait on a Terrace, Bob King, 1962

127
Dr E. G. MacMahon,
1959

office – one of about thirty-five minutes and the other of about
twenty minutes. The final painting was done in four days with
enamels, because the artist felt this medium lends itself to quick
work, and he had a deadline to meet.

After making studies of President Ngo Dinh Diem in
Saigon, Dobell flew to Hong Kong to paint the actual portrait
at the home of *Time*'s Eastern correspondent. On this trip he
kept a diary of sketched impressions which he has used as the
basis for such later paintings as the charming *Sketch of Hong
Kong* and *Impression of Hong Kong*.   *Ill. 116*

As we have seen, Dobell rarely paints his portraits in the
presence of the sitter. With the sitter before him he makes a
series of sketches in pencil, gouache, or oil – often as many as
four or five different studies in different media and of different

128 *Prime Minister Menzies, 1960*

moods. 'Sometimes', he says, 'I move around the head to get the profile. If I only draw a full face there is nothing to tell you how large the nose really is, so I like to get a sculptor's view of the head – then you can make the nose come forward. The more you look at people the more you see in them.'

With the sketches finished he returns to his studio. 'I get the main design from my best study and then I put them away –

at hand, but behind the easel somewhere, so I can go around and refer to them if I have to. But I never work with them in front of me – it constipates me.

'I like to get their real personality and I think you only get that by knowing the person – I try to remember their moods and I keep them in my mind all the time by remembering the things they said to me. Scotty Allan was done completely from memory and the only way I could conjure him up was by talking Scots to myself all the time.' *Ill. 68*

Above all, he wants to capture the personality. About his portrait of Dame Mary Gilmore he said: 'She hasn't a neck exactly like that, but I wanted to get her the way she sits and spouts poetry and looks dreamily into the distance and does this with her hands. That was what I wanted, that gesture, so I had to lengthen the neck to get it.'

There can be no doubt that *Dame Mary Gilmore* is one of his greatest paintings. It was commissioned by the Australian *Ill. 115*

129
The Matriarch,
1967

Book Society in 1955 to commemorate Dame Mary's ninetieth birthday, but it was not finished to Dobell's satisfaction until 1957. Three years later, at the age of ninety-five, she presented it to the Art Gallery of New South Wales because she felt it deserved to be seen by as many people as possible.

'It was extraordinary', she said, when first shown the finished portrait. 'I walked in the door and all I saw were my father's eyes looking at me. I hadn't been thinking about him either. He had been dead for sixty years. The family likeness was in that portrait, yet Dobell never knew any members of my family.'

The ordinary spectator cannot be expected to appreciate it from this point of view, but every observer must be conscious

130 The Titivaters, 1968

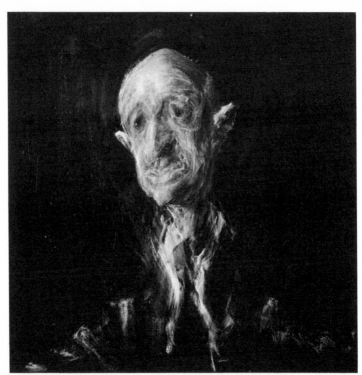

131
The Kindly Man,
1968

of its tremendous dignity. Serene, yet alert, the figure tapers upwards in sharply diminishing proportions. Anyone who has stood at the entrance of a Gothic Cathedral and looked up at the figures carved on the portals will recognize the effect Dobell has achieved in this painting. He has transformed her into a symbol without lessening her reality as an individual – she is both poetess and woman. The stiff, hieratic pose, the formal rhythms of the almost abstract drapery, and the prevailing blue–green harmonies of the colour scheme all lead to the face and concentrate our attention on it.

Twenty years earlier Dobell had begun his career as a portrait painter by a study of faces that had the characteristics of a type. *Mrs South Kensington* is such a one. Now he has learnt the art of endowing the individual with the status of a symbol. The portrait of Dame Mary Gilmore is both a public image and a private image. It is an expression of the things she stood for and the position she occupied, as well as the way she looked and the kind of person she was.

Occasionally the artist meets a personality that challenges his powers of assessment. How else can one explain the fact that within six years he has painted eight different portraits of Helena Rubinstein?

The first sketches were made in April 1957.

'She was a good sitter, but oddly enough, rather diffident and shy – a very nice person with a strong personality. She sat for me twice – for an hour each time in her suite in a Sydney hotel. I made several drawings, and then back in my studio did four or five tiny little oils, all highly finished and about six inches square. From these I finally hit on what I wanted for the big portrait.'

Ill. 118 This big portrait was entered for, and won, the *Australian Women's Weekly* Portrait Prize for 1957, but since then he has Ill. 119 painted a completely different version called *Woman in a Salon* in 1960, and yet another version finished early in 1963. The sketch and the small oil study are earlier versions made in 1957.

Perhaps Dobell's own words can help us understand why the subject has fascinated him so much. He described her as being 'rather diffident and shy' yet with 'a strong personality'. Evidently he sensed opposing characteristics in his sitter's personality and his repeated studies are an attempt to elucidate the mystery.

Certainly, in the majority of them we sense a woman of strong personality who has built an empire in the cosmetics industry. In these the paint is bold, decisive, and vigorous. There is nothing shy or diffident about them. On the contrary, they are assertive to the point of aggressiveness.

The *Woman in a Salon* is different. Every refinement of touch and artifice of colour is used to create a mood of reverie. The room she sits in is already dark with evening shadows. Her damask dress glimmers in the fading light. You would guess

132
The Confection,
1968

that her thoughts were calm and peaceful, yet she holds herself like an actress constantly conscious of the effects she produces. This is the woman whose taste and judgement established a pattern of feminine beauty. The other Helena Rubinstein is the woman who amassed a huge fortune in doing so.

Lydia with Hair in Pins is a figment of Dobell's imagina- *Ill. 124*
tion. No such woman exists. No one modelled for it. Even the dogs were taken from sketches made years ago. Yet she is as vividly alive as one of Dickens most sharply drawn characters

and, being wholly a creature of Dobell's mind, she tells us a great deal about her creator.

To begin with, she is no great beauty – Dobell is rarely interested in conventional beauty. Her morals probably match her looks – Dobell is no moralist. He is only interested in what people are, not in what they should be. There is something fussily sleazy about her. She would be inclined to worry about the wrong things and forget the really important things. She would make sure her hair was curled but would probably forget to wash. Her name according to her creator, is Lydia Dustbin, and she is very fond of dogs. She might very well *Ill. 50* be the heroine of a *Souvenir* grown older still, but still no wiser.

All his formidable technical skill has been used to make her believable. Although he has occasionally worked with enamels he prefers the more traditional techniques and media.

Most of his paintings, and *Lydia* is no exception, are painted with copal varnish as a medium, though he sometimes uses dammar varnish in smaller paintings. *Kanana* was painted with dammar; *Lydia* with copal.

Frequently he will sketch the outlines of his painting in gouache on the dark brown unprimed surface of the hardboard. He corrects his drawing by washing away mistakes with a damp rag, but when it is drawn to his satisfaction he fixes it with a coat of copal. Then he proceeds to build up his painting by laying-in the darker tones and painting the local colour into them. If he loses his colour he will glaze it back on to the surface by using an emulsion made of equal parts of linseed oil, turpentine, and water, and paint into it once again with the copal medium.

In this way he unifies the richly textured surfaces with layers of transparent glazes. He loves the slightly dragging effect of copal. The brush pulls the paint into countless little irregularities like the pores of the skin, or the weave of cloth. It allows him to work over and over the surface, each stroke aiming at an increased subtlety of modelling, or at an enhancement of the colour.

202

In recent years he has delighted in making what he calls 'white drawings'. Colour is reduced to a minimum, and his subject, whether it be a self-portrait, the evocation of an imaginary character or a study of the Sydney Opera House, is conjured out of a network of fine white lines. The brush hovers and darts about the subject like a silver-pointed pencil and evokes the form through an accumulation of a hundred brisk and nervous strokes.

Sometimes his love of Guardi's water-laden skies and vaporous canals finds expression in images of Sydney's Opera House, floating like a dream in an immensity of sky and water.

Ill. 1

Ill. 132

Ill. 133

133 *The Opera House, Sydney, Second version, 1968 (unfinished)*

As time goes by he is less and less inclined to paint actual portraits, but like a great novelist he creates his own characters from the vast storehouse of his observations. These men and women seem no less real than those he has painted from life. They are just as varied, and just as vulnerable. Though the technique is now quite different, these late and brilliant essays in character take us back to the London years when he looked at, remembered, and painted such unforgettable characters as *Mrs South Kensington*, the *Woman in Restaurant*, *The Charlady*, the *Cockney Mother* and *Street Singer*.

In the Queen's Birthday Honours List of June, 1966, he received a knighthood for his contribution to Australian art.

At this point it is tempting to make a final assessment of Dobell's art, but such an attempt would be premature. The artist is still working, and paintings yet unpainted could substantially effect the opinions we would form of his achievement as a whole, and it must always be remembered that works of art can mean different things to different generations. Only the passing of many generations can establish a consensus of opinion that will allot to Dobell his true place in the history of art.

One thing is certain, in Australia today his works are more eagerly sought after than those of any of his contemporaries. His slightest sketches are fought for in the auction rooms, and when pictures change hands they do so at prices one usually associates with old masters.

But whether we agree with him or not, it is fitting to allow the artist the last word.

'I am always worried whether I am doing my best work. I think I have been side-tracked a lot by trying to keep up to date with modernism. I am essentially a traditionalist and I think trying to be a modernist has side-tracked me. I have failed to do my best work.'

Acknowledgements

Above all, the author is indebted to the artist, who answered innumerable questions on many occasions and patiently submitted to a protracted inquisition before a tape recorder.

Most of the illustrations were selected by the artist. Much of the documentation has been facilitated by the copious files placed at my disposal by the artist's friend, Frank Clune, and by the indefatigable energies of Mrs Thelma Clune.

Denis Millen has travelled many thousands of miles to photograph Dobells in widely scattered collections.

I would like to thank the Trustees and Directors of the Art Galleries of Sydney, Brisbane, Melbourne, Adelaide, and Perth, the Director of the Australian War Memorial at Canberra, the Governors of the Stratford-on-Avon Memorial Theatre, and the many private owners who have permitted their paintings to be inspected, photographed and reproduced.

I am also indebted to Ure Smith Pty. Ltd for permission to use their reproductions of the destroyed *Joshua Smith* and the unavailable *Dead Landlord*.

J.G.

List of Illustrations

19   Tired Nippy, 1937
      Oil on cardboard, $25\frac{5}{8} \times 11\frac{5}{8}$ ins
      Private collection

20   Boy Lounging, 1937
      Gouache on strawboard,
      $9\frac{1}{8} \times 8\frac{3}{4}$ ins
      Collection: Art Gallery of New
      South Wales

21   Sketch for Irish Youth, 1935
      Lithographic crayon on paper,
      $14\frac{1}{2} \times 9\frac{1}{4}$ ins
      Private collection

22   Sketch for Irish Youth, 1938
      Oil on cardboard, $10\frac{7}{8} \times 6\frac{3}{4}$ ins
      Private collection

23   Irish Youth, 1938
      Oil on canvas, $21\frac{3}{4} \times 17\frac{1}{8}$ ins
      Private collection

24   The Charlady, 1936
      Oil on canvas on hardboard,
      $13\frac{3}{8} \times 10\frac{3}{8}$ ins
      Private collection

25   Mrs South Kensington, 1927
      Oil on plywood, $14\frac{1}{8} \times 12\frac{1}{4}$ ins
      Collection: Art Gallery of New
      South Wales

26   Sketch for The Cypriot, 1937
      Sepia ink and wash on paper,
      $10\frac{3}{4} \times 10\frac{1}{2}$ ins
      Collection: Australian National
      Gallery, Canberra

27   Boy at the Basin, 1932
      Oil on wooden panel, $16\frac{1}{8} \times 13$ ins
      Collection: Art Gallery of New
      South Wales

28   Toilette, 1936
      Oil on plywood, $13\frac{3}{4} \times 11$ ins
      Private collection

29   The Dead Landlord, 1936
      Oil on canvas, 11×14 ins
      Private collection

30   The Sleeping Greek, 1936
      Oil on canvas on hardboard,
      $15 \times 12\frac{7}{8}$ ins
      Collection: Art Gallery of New
      South Wales

31   The Red Lady, 1937
      Oil on canvas, 32×28 ins
      Collection: Australian National
      Gallery, Canberra

32   Cockney Mother, 1937
      Oil on plywood, $18\frac{1}{4} \times 7\frac{5}{8}$ ins
      Private collection

33   The White Horse Inn, Dorking,
      1935
      Oil on canvas, $13\frac{1}{2} \times 17$ ins
      Private collection

34   Kensington Gardens, 1935
      Oil on hardboard, $6\frac{1}{2} \times 8\frac{1}{4}$ ins
      Collection: National Gallery of
      Victoria

35   Street in Pimlico, 1937
      Oil on pasteboard, $13\frac{1}{2} \times 10\frac{1}{2}$ ins
      Collection: Art Gallery of New
      South Wales

36   A London Bridge, 1936
      Oil on canvas, 16×20 ins
      Collection: Queensland Art Gal-
      lery, Brisbane

37   Street Singer, 1938
      Oil on plywood, $14\frac{3}{8} \times 11\frac{5}{8}$ ins
      Collection: Art Gallery of West-
      ern Australia

38   My Lady Waits, 1937
      Oil on cardboard, $9 \times 7\frac{1}{4}$ ins
      Collection: National Gallery of
      Victoria

59 The Concrete Workers, 1944
Ink on paper, $8\frac{1}{2} \times 6\frac{1}{2}$ ins
Private collection

60 Concrete Consolidation Worker,
Sydney Graving Dock, 1944
Oil on canvas, 10×14 ins
Collection: Australian War
Memorial, Canberra

61 Night Recreation C.C.C. Camp,
1944
Oil on pulpboard, $9\frac{1}{2} \times 11\frac{5}{8}$ ins
Collection: Australian War
Memorial, Canberra

62 Knocking-off Time, Bankstown
Aerodrome, 1944
Oil on canvas, 15×19 ins
Collection: Australian War
Memorial, Canberra

63 The Cypriot, 1940
Oil on canvas, $48\frac{1}{4} \times 48\frac{1}{4}$ ins
Collection: Queensland Art Gal-
lery, Brisbane

64 Portrait of a Boy, 1943
Oil on canvas $28\frac{5}{8} \times 20\frac{7}{8}$ ins
Private collection

65 Study for The Student, 1940
Oil on paper, 17×10 ins
Private collection

66 The Billy Boy, 1943
Oil on canvas, 28×21 ins
Collection: Australian War
Memorial, Canberra

67 Elaine Haxton, 1941
Oil on canvas, $41\frac{1}{2} \times 34\frac{1}{2}$ ins
Collection: Art Gallery of West -
ern Australia

68 Capt. G. U. 'Scotty' Allan, 1941
Oil on hardboard, $25 \times 19\frac{3}{8}$ ins
Private collection

69 The Strapper, 1941
Oil on canvas, 35×26 ins
Collection: Newcastle City Art
Gallery

70 James Cook, 1942
Oil on canvas, $37\frac{1}{2} \times 29$ ins
Private collection

71 Norman Schureck, 1942
Oil on canvas, $10\frac{3}{8} \times 9\frac{5}{8}$ ins
Private collection

72 Study for David Lloyd Jones,
1943
Pencil on paper, $8\frac{1}{2} \times 6\frac{3}{4}$ ins
Collection: National Gallery of
Victoria

73 Sketch for Cement Worker, 1943
Pen and ink on white paper,
$8\frac{7}{8} \times 6$ ins
Private collection

74 Cement Worker, Sydney Grav-
ing Dock, 1944
Oil on pulpboard, $29 \times 19\frac{1}{4}$ ins
Collection: Australian War
Memorial, Canberra

75 Joshua Smith, 1943
Oil on canvas, 48×32 ins
Private collection

76 Brian Penton, 1943
Oil on canvas, $35\frac{1}{2} \times 27\frac{1}{2}$ ins
Private collection

77 Study for Joshua Smith, 1943
Oil on hardboard, $14\frac{1}{8} \times 10\frac{1}{8}$ ins
Private collection

121 Portrait of a Youth, 1954
Oil on hardboard, 48 × 32 ins
Collection: Queensland Art Gallery, Brisbane

122 Rattails, 1959
Oil on hardboard, 19¼ × 14⅝ ins
Private collection

123 Anne Hamer, 1955
Oil on hardboard, 30 × 24 ins
Private collection

124 Lydia with Hair in Pins, 1963
Oil on hardboard, 45¼ × 26⅜ ins
Private collection

125 Portrait of Professor John Anderson, 1961
Oil on hardboard
Private collection

126 Portrait on a Terrace, Bob King, 1962
Oil on hardboard, 21 × 31 ins
Private collection

127 Dr E. G. MacMahon, 1959
Oil on hardboard
Private collection

128 Prime Minister Menzies, 1960
Oil on hardboard, 23⅝ × 19½ ins
Collection: Art Gallery of New South Wales

129 The Matriarch, 1967
Oil on hardboard, 13¾ × 11⅞ ins
Private collection

130 The Titivaters, 1968
Oil on hardboard, 32 × 38 ins
Private collection

131 The Kindly Man, 1968
Oil on hardboard, 22 × 22½ ins
Private collection

132 The Confection, 1968
Oil on hardboard, 24½ × 18½ ins
Private collection

133 The Opera House, Sydney (second version, unfinished), 1968
Oil on hardboard, 43 × 48 ins
Private collection

Index

All references are to page numbers; those in italic indicate illustrations

214